BEYOND EXCEPTION

BEYOND EXCEPTION

New Interpretations of the Arabian Peninsula

AHMED KANNA, AMÉLIE LE RENARD,
AND NEHA VORA

CORNELL UNIVERSITY PRESS
ITHACA AND LONDON

First published 2020 by Cornell University Press

Library of Congress Cataloging-in-Publication Data

Names: Kanna, Ahmed, author. | Le Renard, Amélie, author. |
    Vora, Neha, 1974- author.
Title: Beyond exception : new interpretations of the Arabian Peninsula /
    Ahmed Kanna, Amélie Le Renard, and Neha Vora.
Description: Ithaca : Cornell University Press, 2020. |
    Includes bibliographical references and index.
Identifiers: LCCN 2019042267 (print) | LCCN 2019042268 (ebook) |
    ISBN 9781501750298 (hardcover) | ISBN 9781501750304 (paperback) |
    ISBN 9781501750311 (ebook) | ISBN 9781501750328 (pdf)
Subjects: LCSH: Ethnology—Persian Gulf Region. | Exceptionalism—
    Persian Gulf Region. | Orientalism—Persian Gulf Region. |
    Persian Gulf Region—Civilization—21st century.
Classification: LCC GN640 .K36 2020 (print) | LCC GN640 (ebook) |
    DDC 306.0953—dc23
LC record available at https://lccn.loc.gov/2019042267
LC ebook record available at https://lccn.loc.gov/2019042268

CONTENTS

BEYOND EXCEPTION

Introduction

Ethnography from the Exceptional to the Everyday

AMÉLIE LE RENARD, NEHA VORA, AHMED KANNA

This book grew out of conversations the three of us had over the course of the past several years about ethnography, postcolonial theory, feminism, racialization, and class struggle and how these might conceptually and methodologically relate to the Arabian Peninsula, where we have been conducting field research for the bulk of our careers. There is a frequent recourse to tropes of fantasy and literature, science fiction, and other similar motifs when Western journalists and sometimes even academics seek to explain the Arabian Peninsula to their audiences. Some of these themes draw on Orientalist discursive traditions that reify a divide between West and East, modern and traditional, liberal and illiberal, progressive and savage (Gregory 2004; Lewis and Wigen 1997; Said 1978). Other themes go beyond Orientalism, which is why we choose to talk about "exceptionalism." Representations of the Gulf include, notably, the tropes of hypermodernity and inauthenticity. Our encounter with exoticizing and exceptionalist discourses over the nearly two decades that we have each been conducting fieldwork in the region inspired conversations among the three of us that became the springboard for this book, a reflection on conducting fieldwork within a "field" that is marked by such representations, not only from the outside but also by state discourses, by academic and other "expert" commentary, and by our interlocutors themselves. In this context, we could have focused on deconstructing the exceptionalist representations that circulate about the Arabian Peninsula, or proposing alternative ones. We argue, however, that reflexive ethnographic fieldwork can go further: in this book, we analyze what exceptionalism does, how it is used by various people, and how it helps shape power relations in the societies we study.

Each of us had been reflecting on how our respective academic formations and social positions shaped our own assumptions about fieldwork in the Gulf, and how these assumptions in turn resonated and overlapped with larger ways that the region has been conceptually mapped and imagined, within and without academe—indeed, how it became a region in the first place. These exceptionalist discourses contrasted with the critical discussion on knowledge and power that had become central in Middle East feminist studies in the end of the 1990s (Abu-Lughod 1998, 2001), a field that particularly inspired Amélie's PhD work on young urban women's lifestyles and transforming femininity norms in Riyadh. In the past decades, postcolonial Middle East feminist studies have been reflexive about how to counter stereotypes on women's oppression by showing how imperialism, nationalism, capitalism, and class have contributed to shaping projects of "modernity," "tradition," or "authenticity" that impact gender norms and relations (Abu-Lughod 1998). We also noted how ethnographic work on the region's inhabitants often reified the "peoples and cultures" model (Gupta and Ferguson 1992) that had been heavily critiqued in postcolonial studies, anthropology of empire and modernity, and transnational feminism. Many of these texts highlighted how the subject position of the researcher was integral to the production of knowledge, and advanced more nuanced and reflexive methodologies. These approaches were influential to Neha's original interest in diasporic South Asians in Dubai and her subsequent work on higher education in Doha, projects that explored the power dynamics behind prevailing nationalist, statist, and academic representations of identity and belonging. Issues of politics and representation became intensely salient especially after 9/11 and the subsequent US war on terror and wars in Afghanistan and Iraq, which occurred between the second and fourth years of Ahmed's US-based PhD program in cultural anthropology. They catalyzed his political radicalization to the left, leading to an activist life in revolutionary Marxism in which he began to subject not only Orientalism but also much of the supposedly more "progressive" field of anthropology and academia more generally to a class critique.

As we developed our conversations further and added to their conceptual sophistication, we came to hypothesize that the Gulf was constituted as what Edward Said would call an "imaginative geography." We had many discussions about how much time we spent in our scholarly careers writing against this imaginative geography—or what Lila Abu-Lughod would call "writing against culture"—and about how we struggled at times to make our work legible and our arguments persuasive in contexts, both to area studies scholars and to our disciplinary colleagues, where readers expected the sensational. Thus, one of the main questions for us as ethnographers (Amélie is a French sociologist, Ahmed and Neha are American anthropologists, but our research methods are very similar), and one we hope will help advance debates about ethnographic theory and method, is, What does the persistence of exoticizing accounts mean for conducting fieldwork?[1]

In this book, we explore the question of what it means to conduct ethnography in supposedly exceptional spaces, which have largely been rendered devoid of exactly what ethnographers study: the mundane, everyday aspects of human (and nonhuman) life. What does it mean to conduct research in zones that are imagined to be exceptional to the rest of the world? What does it mean to try to deconstruct exceptionalist tropes while also facing them in the field? And finally, how does the positionality of the researcher in supposedly exceptional places impact the knowledge that is produced?

While Said's *Orientalism* has engendered transformations in many fields of social science, exceptionalist discourses are still common about the Arabian Peninsula. This exceptionalism came to the fore in media and academic coverage of the "crisis" in the Gulf region. In June 2017, on the heels of a heavily publicized visit by President Trump, Saudi Arabia's leadership, along with the governments of the United Arab Emirates (UAE), Bahrain, and Egypt, cut off diplomatic ties with Qatar and initiated a land, air, and sea blockade, based primarily on claims that Qatar was funding terrorist groups, catalyzing a regional foreign policy "crisis." Several other countries followed suit with lessened diplomatic and trade ties with Qatar, while Kuwait's emir and the sultan of Oman stepped in to try to negotiate the growing rift in the Gulf Cooperation Council (GCC) states, which, given their combined petro-wealth, their centrality to air and port traffic, and their strategic location at the seat of Western military operations in the Middle East, left many foreign policy and trade experts concerned about lasting global ripple effects. The tensions between Qatar and its neighbors were so high at the beginning of the crisis that Saudi Arabia and the UAE began deporting Qataris living in those countries, even those married to their citizens, and Iran and Turkey had to airlift food into Qatar, whose only land border (with Saudi Arabia) was—and still is at the time of this writing—closed off. Air traffic between the countries was prohibited for GCC residents, and Qatari media, particularly Al Jazeera, were censored in the "Saudi coalition" states.[2] Soon after, the UAE made any praise of Qatar punishable by fines or jail time. While this blockade effectively ended Qatar's participation in a years-long war on Yemen, the Saudi-led coalition, with the aid of the United States, continued its relentless campaign.

The media and pundit coverage of this tense situation was telling. In general, the Gulf crisis was framed as a "diplomatic spat," a spectacle marked by tropes of exceptionalism and Orientalism that diminished the importance of the Gulf region, its rulers, and, especially, the people who live there. News coverage with such titles as "Under Siege in the Gilded Cage of Qatar" (*The Times*, June 11, 2017) and "Why Qatar Is in the Naughty Corner" (*New York Times*, June 6, 2017) harked back to Thomas Friedman's infamous "tribes with flags" description of the Gulf states and made it hard for readers to take even the better reporting and analysis seriously.[3] One author, an academic writing for a national security and strategy think tank, mixed a *Game of Thrones* analogy with other facile aspersions: Saudi Arabia, the UAE, and Qatar were going on "princely ego trips" and engaging in a "reality show resembling *Dumb and Dumber*"; and, as if the point was not already clear enough, he added: "Who needs a foreign threat when you have careless princes?" (Cordesman 2017). Writing for the *Guardian*, another writer also invoked the comparison to *Game of Thrones* and intoned that diplomatic problems in the GCC were exceptionally difficult to solve because they were "personal as well as political" (unlike, one assumes, in the liberal West, where politics are rational and only about policy). Another variation on this "irrational Gulf" theme is the assertion, in the same article, that Gulf political conflicts are simply "a long running family feud," a reflection of "the fractious world of Middle Eastern politics, where absolute monarchs trade on their bloodline and piety," where "family dissent is often stalled by dispersing privilege and cash" (Ramesh 2017).[4] Two years into the Gulf crisis, the rhetoric has toned down, but news outlets still cast the blockade of Qatar in terms of a masculinist family feud in which Qatar is a little brother to Saudi Arabia, effectively isolating the conflict from larger international interests and forces.

The coverage of the Gulf crisis recuperates several exceptionalist representations that have been central in media as well as in academic discourses in the past decades. When we began our respective dissertation fieldwork projects, Amélie in Saudi Arabia and Ahmed and Neha in Dubai in the early 2000s, we encountered and to varying degrees indeed carried with us similar, if not identical, portrayals. We mention a few examples of such representations here; others are developed throughout the book. Beside classical Orientalist tropes insisting on religion or tradition as sole explanations for people's conduct in the Middle East, the rentier state theory has for long been a dominant paradigm in social science on the Arabian Peninsula. This theory could be summed up in a principle: "no representation without taxation," sometimes referred to as a "ruling bargain" (Davidson 2008). According to this theory, Gulf citizens have traded political rights for social ones: access to various state benefits and subsidies that are derived from the "rent" of oil prospects (or sale of oil). The rentier state theory raises several issues, as it separates oil-rich countries from other states that rely on resource extraction or structure their economies around social welfare (Kanna 2011; Mitchell 2011; Vora 2013a). It separates Gulf oil economies from their important role in supporting global capitalism and its entanglements with liberal democratic state formation. And it has contributed to constructing the image of Gulf nationals as apathetic, materialistic, and backward while rendering the colonial and imperial history of the Arabian Peninsula and the oil industry invisible. Rentier state analyses also tend to ignore gender, class struggle, racialized labor division, and state repression. In the wake of this theory, the beginning of oil exploitation is often seen as the beginning of history in the Arabian Peninsula, as if nothing had happened there since the seventh century (and before). Another widespread exceptionalist representation of the Gulf considers the city as a frightening fantasy, avant-garde in terms of consumerism and slavery-like exploitation, a society without freedom and without middle classes, divided up into a rich leisure class and an army of quasi slaves.[5]

These representations of Saudi Arabia, the UAE, and Qatar—the three countries we focus on in this book—evacuate society of the social while rendering "culture" as fixed in timeless ideas of bedouins, Islam, indentured labor, and gender repression (Abu-Lughod 1991). This kind of history, politics, and culture writing explains the transformations of Gulf societies by locating all power and agency within local rulers and Western consultants (see also Vitalis 2007). Doing this erases the long and complex histories of class, anti-colonial, and nationalist struggles that have marked the region as much as any other postcolonial context, and removes the agency and complex role of both citizens and noncitizens in forming the fabric of Gulf societies. While indeed many people living and working in the Arabian Peninsula exist in states of economic, legal, and gendered/sexualized precarity, the Gulf itself is not a liminal space, an empty desert canvas as many "starchitects" have claimed for building their dreamscapes (Kanna 2011), nor a land of constant uncertainty and "shifting sands" (the metaphors in scholarly work abound just as frequently as in the journalism we noted above). Rather, the liminal existences of some (not all) Gulf residents resonate with broader global shifts: growing urbanism in East and Central Asia; increased transnational migra-tion of students, workers, and corporations between Africa and China; the rise of a postcolonial middle class while the rift between rich and poor also gets wider in South Asia and Latin America; the international division of care labor between the Philippines and Europe (Parreñas 2000); and a move away from industrialism to knowledge economy development in the Middle East. In other words, what happens in Gulf cities can be compared to, and is connected with, what happens in other global cities all over the world.

In our individual work to date, we have critiqued how remnants of Ori-entalism are recuperated in much of the literature about the Arabian Penin-sula (and in state projects of heritage and legitimacy), producing Gulf excep-tionalism through uncritical accounts of authoritarian power, illiberal state-society relations, ethnic citizenship, women's oppression, and exploit-ative migration policies (Kanna 2011; Le Renard 2014a; Vora 2013a). More-over, we have attended to the ways Orientalism, as a dominant framework that persists in discourses on the region (though by no means is it the only one), plays a crucial role in ongoing imaginative geographies and political economies of race, class, gender, and empire in contemporary Arabian Pen-insula. Here, we build on those interventions to move beyond the discursive frame by thinking through not only the writing process but also the process of conducting fieldwork itself, and how exceptionalizing frameworks influence every aspect of knowledge production for ethnographers, their interlocutors, and the built environment itself.

In *Colonising Egypt*, Timothy Mitchell (1991) explores how European travelers to the Middle East came with preformed representations of space, culture, and symbolic ordering, thereby "rediscovering," and in turn attempting to reorder, places that were already known to them through previous circulations of knowledge, particularly the discourses and aesthetics of modernity and its others. It was in the disjuncture between the orderly chaos of cities like Cairo or Algiers that was premapped onto the European imaginary, and the actual cities themselves—where streets had no names, where boundaries between spatial functions were unclear, and where the edges of the cities were undefined—that colonial urbanization and world making took place. In many ways, this colonial optic and its imaginaries of Middle Eastern space have intensified and sharpened as they have moved into twenty-first-century accounts of Arabian Peninsula urbanism. It is unlikely that a traveler or scholar will be "discovering" Dubai, Doha, or Riyadh, for example, but rather arrive with a preformed imaginary that is then confirmed by the spaces where they go and the people that they meet there. News articles and one-off research projects about Gulf cities are often interchangeable in their representations of culture, people, power, and space, as were the products of the Orientalist repertoire that Mitchell and Said have explored. More recently, the mega-development coverage of Dubai has also become transposable in its spectacular tropes to Doha and Abu Dhabi.

Encountering the Arabian Peninsula for the first time, we did not experience the rediscovery—even though we had expected it—that we described above. Instead, we found rather immediately that not only did we not know our place in Gulf cities' social and geographical ordering, but also that this ordering was not as clear to us as we had assumed prior to arrival. How does access to knowledge of everyday life get circumscribed by exceptionalizing accounts, which obscure the complexities of these incredibly diverse, historically and geopolitically significant spaces? And what does the persistence of exceptionalist tropes on the Gulf reveal about power relations in academia?

While critiques of Orientalism and other forms of civilizational representation and discourse are now familiar to many audiences in the humanities and social sciences, the term "exceptionalism" needs further discussion. By Gulf exceptionalism, we are referring not only to representational practices but also to the ways that global political-economic and cultural connections, and histories of imperialism and capitalism, have been de-emphasized and often erased in knowledge production on the Arabian Peninsula, as well as financial, military, and diplomatic engagement. Therefore, exceptionalism calls forward a multilayered way of thinking about the effects of representation, which are embedded in state projects, migrant narratives, and heritage making—thus, there is no way to claim a hegemonic "Western" site of production of exceptionalism when it comes to the Gulf region, although we are interested in highlighting how this exceptionalism both obscures and advances US and European imperial interests in the region, certain forms of global capitalism, and white supremacy.

As we discuss later and in more detail in the remainder of the book, the persistence of Gulf exceptionalism owes not least to the way this part of Asia was incorporated into a British- and later US-dominated capitalist global order in the nineteenth and twentieth centuries. For this reason, postcolonial approaches that question the relation between the colonial past and the globalized present, without reducing it to either rupture or continuity (S. Ahmed 2000, 11), have been useful to us. While the complex history of imperialism in the Arabian Peninsula is beyond the scope of this book, it is important to mention here a few elements for readers unfamiliar with the Peninsula. The region was partly under Ottoman control until the early twentieth century. Beginning in the nineteenth century, Great Britain established protectorates on the coast to secure the maritime routes to India, and this process had important implications for the reconfiguration of political power, its territorialization, and circulations between the Arabian Peninsula and India. As for the Saudi emirate, a treaty signed in 1915 between Ibn Saud and Great Britain conceded sovereignty for protection; a second treaty, in 1927, declaring Ibn Saud's complete independence, did not avoid strong forms of dependence toward Great Britain until 1945, when Saudi Arabia became, to some extent, "America's Kingdom" (Vitalis 2007). Most of the various struggles against imperialism that took place in the Arabian Peninsula, from strikes in Saudi-American Aramco to nationalist protests in Abu Dhabi, were repressed and did not lead to significant breaks in the relations between the governments and their imperial "protectors." There were, however, various transnational interconnections among struggles in Saudi Arabia, Oman, and Yemen, as "counternarratives" by historians and political scientists reveal (Al-Rasheed and Vitalis 2008; Bonnefoy 2018; Carapico 2004; Vitalis 2007).

Today, the GCC states play the role of bulwarks in an American-led "axis of reaction" in the larger Middle East and North Africa (MENA) region. Relatedly, Gulf exceptionalism has articulated with the official historiographies of Saudi Arabia, the UAE, Bahrain, Qatar, and, to some extent, Kuwait to help prop up repressive ruling families whose power and legitimacy are contested by their own people, marginalizing, erasing, and suppressing countermovements and various forms of resistance within their borders and in neighboring countries, as the current Saudi-led, American-backed war on Yemen shows once more (Al Kuwari 2012; Beaugrand 2017; Bonnefoy and Louër 2015; Bsheer 2018; Carapico 2016; Matthiesen 2013, 2014; Shehabi and Owen-Jones 2015). The officially sanctioned picture of the Gulf as (bedouin) Arab, Islamic, capitalist, traditional, religious, and patriarchal is not, as exceptionalist discourse would lead us to believe, an unbiased description of the supposed cultural essence of the societies in the region, but a result of the massive and long-term, often bloody, struggle, in which the most reactionary forces in the region, with the assistance of international reaction (mainly in the form of Britain and the United States), have, at least for the moment, triumphed. In referring to Gulf exceptionalism, we seek to highlight the politics of Gulf culture discourses and imagined geographies of Gulf identity, and also to bring to the foreground the role of struggle and resistance in the making of the contemporary Arabian Peninsula.

More broadly, this exceptionalizing framework helps reinforce a neocolonial vision of the world, opposing modernity and tradition, progress and backwardness, civilization and savagery (Mohanty 1984). Such binaries about the Gulf are used in opportunistic ways by political leaders in North America and Europe to support their Gulf counterparts and/or legitimize imperial policies in this, the time of the now two decades long war on terror; but they also are utilized by many of our interlocutors and by state officials in the Arabian Peninsula as well. These discourses and their effects not only need deconstruction, but here in this book we make them an important site of ethnographic inquiry *on the ground*.

While many of the exceptionalizing tropes of the Gulf persist in the scholarly and journalistic work on the region, the fieldwork process itself, by contrast, has changed significantly over the past two decades. It has become easier to get research permissions and access to many places, even if it depends on subjects, countries, and researchers' nationalities and gender.[6] Many researchers have developed projects on various aspects of Gulf societies; some of them have even received funding from public institutions based in the Gulf, such as Qatar Foundation, to do so. This has required Gulf governments to become more transparent in their research visa processes and less arbitrary in detaining researchers for conducting fieldwork they might deem controversial.[7] While experiences vary across countries and institutions, academics associated with Western universities, which have seen a dramatic rise in the past decade, have discussed experiencing increased academic freedom. The influx of universities into the Gulf region, many of which are US and other Western branch campuses and partnerships, has also increased the number of academics and researchers on the ground. Several researchers who have published in the past few years were able to conduct fieldwork in cities where the cost of living is high while teaching at various public and private universities that have developed in the past decades (Ahmad 2017; Menoret 2014; Peutz 2011). State institutions have allowed research projects dealing with sensitive issues such as migration, media, gender, religious practices, and political activism, just to give a few examples (Gardner 2010). This goes hand in hand with their own development goals, which are focused on knowledge economy development and include investments of billions of dollars into research and development sectors, especially in science, technology, engineering, and mathematics (STEM) fields, but also funding research and publishing on heritage, culture, architecture, migration, gender, and other areas that require ethnographic expertise. This dynamic has been reinforced with the war situation affecting several MENA countries, including in the Arabian Peninsula and Yemen, leading some researchers to conduct fieldwork in the Gulf for feasibility (Inhorn 2015). As a consequence, research on Gulf societies covers many more subjects than it has in the past; the field has expanded, has become more complex, and has also become more visible in Middle East and discipline-specific MENA conferences. Geopolitical tensions between GCC countries, however, along with crackdowns on activists, have added to the already fraught political conditions for citizens in particular in several Gulf countries, which further highlights disparities related to research and mobility based on nationality, racialized identity, religion, gender, and other factors.

It is undeniable that the relative ease of access to the Gulf over the past two decades, at least for US-based scholars, including the growth of US universities, is connected to US hegemony in the region, an echo of earlier periods of American anthropology in which Morocco and Yemen featured disproportionately in ethnographic work. Indeed, as we discuss extensively in this book, US hegemony and its project of promoting a capitalist order that serves the interests of North Atlantic Treaty Organization (NATO) countries have themselves shaped research agendas on the region, conditioned inclusions and erasures of particular topics (e.g., race and class), and helped preform the region in imaginative mappings and academic logics. Similarly, imperial logics shape research agendas on the Arabian Peninsula in European countries, which are important political and commercial (asymmetric) "partners" of Gulf states,[8] while the development of Gulf studies in several contexts also echoes the proliferation of social science programs in Gulf universities and research centers.

Gulf Ethnography and Its Interventions

The increase over the past ten to fifteen years in interest by qualitatively oriented social scientists has represented a shift from the previous domination of work on the Arabian Peninsula by policy analysts and others operating under a more international relations framework—or "oil and security." While the latter still represents a large proportion of scholarly output, the more recent surge in qualitative research nevertheless portends a major shift away from the more positivistic work under the rubric of traditional geopolitics. Qualitative research in anthropology, geography, history, and sociology has offered a set of important de-exceptionalizing interventions to which we seek to contribute with this book. These interventions not only expand our empirical knowledge, adding detailed and nuanced ethnographic and historical analyses of generally understudied or ignored cases, but also provide theoretical openings for reimagining research in and on the region. Below, we identify some of the most significant impacts of scholarship on knowledge of the Arabian Peninsula while acknowledging that we cannot be exhaustive.

From Area to Ocean

There has been a dramatic shift in the past decade, with the influence of Indian Ocean studies on anthropology and history, in the way that the

Arabian Peninsula region is understood by ethnographers and in the types of research projects, particularly around migration, that are becoming central within the burgeoning field of Gulf studies. Not only has this work redefined what the Gulf means as an arena for social scientific research, but it has pushed scholars to move the conversation beyond state-centric policy frameworks, which tend to be dominated by theories of the rentier state and presumptions of top-down power relations that both erase migrants from society and homogenize and devalue the agency of citizens (Vora and Koch 2015). Moving away from territorially bound, state-scale research toward tracing Indian Ocean and other networks of imperial history and contemporary exchange allows us to access the rich cosmopolitanism of the region. The trade networks across the Western and Eastern Indian Ocean reveal religious, kinship, cultural, legal, and linguistic exchanges that have influenced what is considered *khaleeji* tradition today (Bishara 2017; Fuccaro 2009; Ho 2007; Khalifa 2006; Lowe 2015; Mathew 2016; Onley 2007). This allows scholars to better interrogate state projects that attempt to erase multiculturalism rather than take them at face value, through museums and heritage sites. And this approach also allows for a more nuanced understanding of Islam as dynamic, transnationally inflected, hybrid, and interpretive rather than statically embedded within the rule of law (Ahmad 2017; Al Rasheed 2016; Limbert 2010; Menoret 2011).

In particular, scholars who have conducted research among migrants from South and Southeast Asia have led the charge in shifting our perceptions of Gulf geography as one that needs to be thought of within a postcolonial context that is linked to British imperial histories as well as contemporary transnational conditions of labor migration (Coles and Walsh 2010; Gamburd 2000; Gardner 2010; Khalaf and Al Kobaisi 1999; P. Leonard 2008; Nagy 2008; Osella and Osella 2006; Thiollet and Vignal 2016; Vora 2013a). Such approaches allow us to compare Gulf societies with other postcolonial contexts and to identify interconnections through circulations of people and cultural practices, as well as of ruling strategies and forms of protest. They shed light on how imperial logics have informed the hierarchies that shape contemporary Gulf cities. British imperialism's racialized capitalist logics and social science apparatus along with ruling elites produced bounded groups that were either "indigenous" or "foreign," and justified a stratified system of employment as well as proxy rule. Meanwhile, American oil interests imported their legacies of forced labor and racial segregation to the Arabian oil fields and reproduced civilizational and Orientalist discourses of both "natives" and nonwhite foreign workers (Coles and Walsh 2010; Khayyat, Khayyat, and Khayyat 2018; Knowles 2007; Kothari 2006; P. Leonard 2008, 2010; Mitchell 2011; Vitalis 2007). The ethnoracial stratification and forms of patronage and exploitation that we see today are in fact transnational historical assemblages that allow Westerners, and especially whites, along with other elites, to expect and enjoy preferential treatment and self-segregation in the Gulf. Anthropologists have also turned to the question of Western and white "expatriate" experiences in the Gulf, exploring both how they are complicit in reinforcing these structures of ethnoracial hierarchy and how they are impacted by the constraints of noncitizenship, the surveillance state, and migrant sponsorship regulations (Coles and Walsh 2010; Cosquer 2018; Kanna 2014; Le Renard 2016, 2017, 2019a; Vora and Kanna 2018; Walsh 2010).

By highlighting the Indian Ocean as a source for not only people but also cultural resources that shape the vibrancy of various urban spaces in the Gulf, ethnographers have challenged the idea that these are empty deserts devoid of social exchange and everyday life, both for citizens—who are heterogeneous and have histories that trace to the east and the west of the Arabian Sea—and for the dozens of nationalities that currently call places such as Dubai, Kuwait City, and Manama home. This scholarship helps us see how the Arabian Peninsula has been a crossroads of human mobility, religious and cultural exchange, and trade for several centuries, making it impossible to consider it a backwater of the world, or parse its people and their daily lives into binary opposition with the West. The region has been engaged with projects of capitalism, modernity, and liberalism from their inception (Bsheer 2017; Mathew 2016; Mitchell 2011; Vora 2018).

Mundane Migration

The high level of migration to the Gulf region since the 1960s, especially from South Asia, has inspired a body of sociological and economics work that tracks remittances, migration patterns, changes in the home country household and village, and other large-scale impacts that can be quantitatively summarized. Much of this work has been done from the perspective of sending states, particularly India, but there has been work as well on Africa, East Asia, and the Middle East (Adelkhah 2001; Diederich 2005; Malecki and Ewers 2007; Marchal 2005; Rahman 2001; Sekher 1997). Given the amount with which India relies on both trade with and remittances from the Gulf, it is not surprising that the state as well as academics are interested in this large-scale phenomenon. It also is not surprising that the Gulf appears—to Indian and non-Indian academics, as well as to journalists—as an exceptional case of global migration, owing to the sheer number of migrants who reside there, as well as their imbrication in what is called the *kafala* system of migrant sponsorship.

Kafala is a temporary nonimmigrant employer-based sponsorship system, offering no path to citizenship or permanent residency. Because most writing on migration within English-language academia, and certainly within anthropology and related fields, has been dominated by US and European models of immigration (i.e., naturalization, family reunification, and assimilation) that have produced many forms of exclusion, kafala appears to reify the Gulf as distinct and nonmodern. It also places migrants into categories of being where they exist solely as *homo economicus* and overly exploited, making it difficult to see the complexity of their daily lives in the Gulf, their affect and belonging, and their forms of pleasure and leisure (Ahmad 2011). However, "illiberal" migration policies—which aim to deport new migrants before they can seek asylum, or to make sure that "guest workers" do not stay after the end of their contract—are common in today's world, and migrant life in the Gulf, as many ethnographers have shown through their research, is not very different qualitatively than it is elsewhere (Ahmad 2017; Buckley 2013; Koch 2016; Vora 2014b). This work makes migration less sensationalistic and humanizes the Gulf migrant, and also makes working-class struggles visible while linking them to those in other places (Buckley 2013; Hanieh 2011; Khalaf and Al Kobaisi 1999). State policing of foreign residents is also similar to what happens in other contexts, all the more as some Gulf states are engaged in intense cooperation with Western states in terms of controlling populations (Lori 2011, 2012).

By highlighting both the complexity and the ordinariness of migrant lives, they no longer can be reduced to masses of voiceless "bachelor" workers. Exceptionalist representations of migration in the Gulf have been quick to latch onto the male construction worker and female domestic worker as tropes of exploitation, leaving little room to explore their nuanced accounts of migration choices, kinship and intimacy, and challenges both in their home countries and in the Gulf. Ethnographic work on these and other working-class populations, especially that which looks at their role in social reproduction, intimacy, and the dynamics of gender and sexuality in the region, goes far in underlining their agency while also documenting their difficult working conditions (Ahmad 2017; De Regt 2010; Mahdavi 2016). One notable example is *Everyday Conversions* by Attiya Ahmad, which explores migrant South Asian women's decisions to convert to Islam within the context of their everyday housework and intimacies of family life and role in social reproduction of Kuwaiti citizens. Unpacking layers of migrant women's storytelling, Ahmad's text refuses a quick judgment of either coercion or awakening to Islam. Rather, becoming Muslim is inextricably tied to experiences of migration, family left behind, new friends and kin made in Kuwait, and particularly the Islamic *da'wa* center and the women who move in and out of it as they also move between South Asia and the Gulf in their lived journeys to establish better lives for themselves and their families.

Complicating Citizenship

Interdisciplinary work that combines anthropology and sociology with legal studies, historiography, genealogical work, feminist and queer theory, museum studies and archaeology, and a range of other fields has given us a more heterogeneous and even contradictory picture of Gulf citizenship than in previous generations. Gulf societies, even if we take this term to be coterminous with citizenry of the GCC (which we do not), it turns out, are not ethnically homogenous, politically docile, uniformly wealthy, inherently patriarchal, or religiously conservative.

Interdisciplinary ethnographies on Saudi Arabia, Kuwait, Oman, and the UAE, for instance, have deconstructed the exceptionalist image of all Arab Gulf nationals as rich and apathetic. In Saudi Arabia, for example, not all groups have benefited in the same ways from the state's formation and oil rent. While several works have underlined the social downgrading of "bedouins," other groups have been structurally excluded, such as the descendants of slaves, though this subject has remained until now under-researched. The spread of consumerism as a social norm has both transformed and reinforced class hierarchies (Altorki and Cole 1989; Le Renard 2014a; Menoret 2014) while development projects have increased the state's control over the population (Jones 2011). Political activism has also been transformed, and ethnographic works have explored both the complex and diverse modalities of activism referring to Islam, and other, less visible ways to question, transgress, and contest the social and political order (Al Rasheed 2016; Le Renard 2014a; Menoret 2005, 2011). In Kuwait, Oman, and the UAE, similar processes of urban high modernism have gone hand in hand with state control of populations, reification and opposition of "modern" (i.e., Western-oriented, consumerist) and "traditional" identities and class hierarchies, consumerism and privatization, while also generating unexpected refractions and resistances (Al Nakib 2016; Kanna 2011; Limbert 2010).

Studying the region prior to European imperialism has allowed scholars to unpack contemporary projects of nationalism and denaturalize concepts and categories, like the tribe, that had become a priori assumptions in state and academic discourses (Willis 2013). While these postcolonial frameworks have highlighted how the projects of white supremacy and Orientalism shaped the naturalized knowledge of Gulf "peoples and cultures," as we explored above, it is also important to note that there are non-Western racializations and forms of stratification at work in the Arabian Peninsula as well, linked to notions of indigenous Arabness, to legacies of African slavery, to geopolitics, and to forms of Islamic genealogy as it is used and reinterpreted by postcolonial states (Limbert 2014). Nadav Samin (2015), for example, shows how the Saudi state has participated in creating the fixation on "tribal names" among national citizens by making their mention compulsory on ID cards, which has reinforced social hierarchies based on genealogy.

Exceptionalist discourse represents citizen women in the Arabian Peninsula as oppressed because of "ancient" patriarchal traditions and/or obscurantist interpretations of Islam. These representations are not limited to the Gulf. Rather, they are part of broader Orientalist imaginations of gender and tradition in the Middle East, which are related to colonial history (Abu-Lughod 1998; L. Ahmed 1992). However, their deployment on the Arabian Peninsula is particularly unchallenged in the media, especially about Saudi Arabia, often portrayed as the worst country in the world in terms of women's rights. Anthropologists have for several decades deconstructed the essentialist discourse on Saudi so-called traditions and conservatism regarding gender by documenting how sedentarization and urbanization conducted by the state in the context of the oil boom have impacted women's activities and roles. The first generation has often suffered from these changes, becoming more dependent on men and less mobile, as the ethnographic work of Salwa Al-Khateeb (2008, 273–301), conducted in a *hijra* (a village-camp built to settle nomadic populations) in the 1980s, shows. Following generations have accessed new opportunities in terms of education and work while experiencing different constraints in terms of domesticity, conjugality, and consumerism (Almana 1981; Altorki and Cole 1989). Various works on gender in the Gulf have pursued this deconstruction by showing how leaders have used the "woman question" to define national identities in these states, how the question has become central to political debates between different currents of thought, and how it is marked by imperial incursions in postcolonial states. Far from being passive, many women have participated in these debates in the past decades, with diverse points of view; some of them are central political figures (Al-Mughni 2001; Al-Rasheed 2013; Arebi 1994; Bristol-Rhys 2010; Le Renard 2011, 2014a). Other works have shown how policies on gender, sexuality, and reproduction are to be understood in relation to national ideologies and imaginaries (Bristol-Rhys and Osella 2016; Hasso 2010; Inhorn 2015). While exceptionalist discourse represents women as unidimensional, identifying solely as women and oppressed because of their gender, this category is shaped by power relations in terms of class, race, nation, and sexuality. Dialoguing with queer studies, a few works shed light on subversions of national (heteronormative) models of femininity and masculinity through nonbinary subjectivities, and analyze specifically the identification of many Emiratis and Saudis as *buyah* (from "boy"), a word that evokes various forms of nonbinary/transgender self-presentations (Al-Qasimi 2011; Le Renard 2014a).

Complicating citizenship by attending to race, class, gender, and sexuality has produced a much richer understanding of what lived experience for GCC passport holders means, moving us beyond ideas of welfare recipients under rentier structures who are bought off by "ruling bargain" (Davidson 2008). This has also allowed scholars to start taking citizen voices seriously as *political* agents (Ulrichsen 2014), as well as to think about the fuzziness of the boundaries between citizen and noncitizen, such as the impacts of state policies on *bidoon* (stateless) populations, for example (Beaugrand 2017; Lori 2011).

Intimacies of Residency

In her groundbreaking ethnography about Kuwaiti society, Longva (1997) identified three important, but not rigid, vectors of division in Gulf society:

citizen/noncitizen, Arab/non-Arab, and Muslim/non-Muslim. This was one of the first texts to consider the experiences of migrants alongside those of citizens, as most ethnographic and other scholarly work until then (and even to this day) not only represented the frontier between nationals and foreigners as impassable but took on either one or the other topic. Thus "Gulf migration" literature has generally evolved separately from work on "Gulf society" (read nationals only). But several studies have shown how the "anti-integration" policies of most GCC states have not prevented many foreign residents from identifying with the cities and countries they live in (Koch 2015; Thiollet 2010; Vora 2013a). In her ethnography of the sociability of Arab youths in Abu Dhabi, Laure Assaf (2017) shows how identifications in terms of generation and urban belonging may go beyond the citizen/noncitizen divide. Other works show that the boundaries of national citizenship may not be as clear as they seem: for instance, Amin Moghadam's (2013) study of the Iranian diaspora in Dubai questions the frontier between Iranian passport holders and Emirati passport holders of Iranian descent. While the national/foreigner divide is a central hierarchy in Gulf societies—as in many other societies where "migrants" do not have the same rights as "nationals"—this divide should not be naturalized. In reality, the boundary between national and foreigner is blurred and conflicted. Legal histories show us that the parameters of citizenship have always been shifting, and have never been as exclusive as currently presumed. In addition, intermarriage of citizen men (and some women), along with the naturalization of several populations (including manumitted slaves), reveals a long history of multiethnic, multilingual, and other cosmopolitan intimacies in the Arabian Peninsula (Ahmad 2017; Breteau 2019; Crystal 1995; Limbert 2014). And, scholars who work on domestic labor, like Ahmad, whom we profiled above, have pointed out that social reproduction of the citizenry entails intimacies at the most basic level between citizens and noncitizens, which are so readily dismissed because the domestic sphere goes understudied in most scholarly work.

Ethnographers who have focused on spaces where nationals and nonnationals have increased opportunities to interact in the public sphere, such as the workplace and in schools, have brought attention to how hierarchies are reproduced and challenged or reconfigured. This highlights how categories of national and nonnational are not preexisting but develop relationally and are shifting and porous. All three of us, for example, have conducted work in these areas. Ahmed's and Amélie's research in Emirati and Saudi workplaces showcases how even though GCC nationals are uniquely privileged by the welfare states of which they are citizens, they also experience disprivilege when multinational businesses target "talent" in ways that privilege Euro-American passports and reproduce an image of whiteness as expertise (Kanna 2014; Le Renard 2014b). And Neha's research in newly established private universities in the UAE and Qatar has shown how national and foreign resident students renegotiate identities when they learn to interact with each other as peers, leading to both conflict and friendship while also creating new belongings and politicizations for diasporic young people (Vora 2013a, 2015, 2018). Rethinking "society" in the Gulf that includes all residents should not constitute "critical" Gulf studies but a normative entry point. Unfortunately, the exceptionalist discourses have made this entry point one that still requires diligence on the part of committed scholars.

Critical Urbanism

Architects and urban planners, especially Western-trained ones, have been centrally involved in Gulf cities going back at least a half century, to the early days of the oil boom and even before. While there is still a small ethnographic literature on cities, urban planning, and architecture in the region, such work is indeed expanding our conceptualization of what the Gulf and Arabian Peninsula are while simultaneously de-exceptionalizing them. Echoing Brazilian state discourses on Brasilia's centrality to the state's twin projects of nationalism and modernism (Holston 1989), statesmen in the Middle East, especially in the oil-producing states, saw their capitals as incubators and catalysts for their nation-states' entry into postwar capitalist modernity. The newly independent Iraqi state's commissioning in the late 1950s of signature projects by famous modernists such as Le Corbusier, Walter Gropius, Frank Lloyd Wright, Alvar Aalto, and Gio Ponti is perhaps the most prominent example. The Arabian Peninsula, however, was no exception. As Pascal Menoret (2014) has shown in *Joyriding in Riyadh*, Saudi leaders, in conversation with US cold war advisers, hired prominent modernist architect Constantinos Doxiadis to help modernize and expand Riyadh in the early 1970s. Doxiadis's Riyadh master plan was a typical synthesis of modernist and cold war logics, what Menoret terms "containment urbanism," meant to address what cold warriors, both Saudi and American, saw as a key problem of many newly independent (or in Saudi Arabia's case, newly wealthy) global south nation-states: how to ensure that rural migrants to cities came under the hegemony of US-inspired values of consumerism, suburbia, and private property and away from more politically radical currents (Menoret 2014, 69; see also Huber 2013). Doxiadis had taken his experience working in Baghdad on so-called urban hamlets composed of private detached homes, celebrated by the *New York Times* as "anti-communist devices," and applied it to Riyadh. These devices were designed to "save" Iraq's rural-urban migrants from communism, according to Doxiadis, because they reinforced the "tribal" and "ancestral" Arab structures of Iraqi society (Menoret 2014, 70).

Today, Arabian Peninsula cities are taking shape in new political-economic and global terrains, under logics of neoliberal and consumer-oriented urbanisms. Discourses of planners of Dubai, Doha, Riyadh, and other cities in the region may lean more toward notions of consumer well-being than the management of "problematic" populations or cold war ideologies than they used to, but the influence of an imperialist West is still an important factor. Since the end of the Cold War, the Gulf region has become even more important to a financialized, neoliberal political economy dominated by the United States (Hanieh 2011). Cities such as Dubai, Doha, Abu Dhabi, and to a lesser extent Kuwait City are positioned by liberal Western discourses as Western oriented, business friendly, and palatable to Western expatriates and tourists, while local elites to a large degree continue to be positioned as outside of liberalism and as hyper consumers exceeding liberal propriety and the supposed puritanism of capitalist discipline. What is perhaps new, and ostensibly a complication on the narrative of Gulf exceptionalism, is that the discourse on Gulf urbanism today seems to be a reversal of Orientalist ideas. Instead of representing backwardness and "tribalism," Gulf cities such as Doha and Dubai are often invoked by planners and architects as hypermodern laboratories of urban formal experimentation (Koolhaas 2006; for critical perspectives, see MacNeill 2009; Ramos 2010; Kanna 2011; Elsheshtawy 2013; Ramos and Rowe 2013). This is a clear example of why we distinguish between Orientalism and exceptionalism in this book. While these discourses of the hypermodern Gulf often reject Orientalist images of the region, the result is still an exceptionalizing discourse that erases or, at best, oversimplifies a more complex story in which various classes, strata, and formations (of, for example, rent-seeking local elites and architects) struggle to define these cities as places to live, spaces to commodify, objects to plan, and so on. A critical, ethnographic perspective on the Arabian Peninsula clearly highlights the ways that urban phenomena in the region, since at least the mid-twentieth century, are far from being exceptional and are very much part of imperial, capitalist, and global histories and ongoing processes (Al-Nakib 2016; Doherty 2017; Elsheshtawy 2009; Günel 2014, 2019; Kanna 2011, 2014; Menoret 2014).

Outline of the Book

The conversation we present here through our individual and collective voices builds on the important scholarship by ethnographers and other scholars of the Arabian Peninsula, who have engaged with the complexities of social processes in the region and contributed to new understandings of, among others, identity and identification, belonging, and reimagining the region as an arena of dynamic, everyday political struggles. The book begins with, and is in large part a problematization of, the trope of arrival in ethnographic writing. The first chapter, "Space, Mobility, and Shifting Identities in the Constitution of the 'Field,'" cowritten by the three of us, is most explicit in questioning narratives of arrival and the ways that they preform the field as a space and object of ethnographic study. The second, third, and fourth chapters, written, respectively, by Amélie, Neha, and Ahmed, elaborate specific themes and questions related to our de-exceptionalizing project, and move beyond the problematic of arrival to grappling with specificities of how exceptionalizing discourses condition possibilities for ethnographic knowledge and the political critique that, we argue, is an inherent part of ethnographic labor.

Arrival is a critical narrative device in ethnographic writing precisely because it marks the position of outsiders immersing themselves into the field—a field where social order is supposedly more objectively accessible to the participant observer than to the "natives" themselves, and this trope has continued into even the most cutting-edge ethnographies and novel definitions of fieldwork. But who are the natives in a city where the moment Neha steps off the plane she needs to access her rusty Hindi rather than newly learned Arabic, where her diasporic community is not a minority or a neighborhood but the city as a whole? What is foreign and what is not when Ahmed experiences neither his name nor his physical appearance as marked? What kind of outsiders were we when some of us felt more comfortable walking through certain neighborhoods of Dubai than we felt walking through the hallways of our universities and hometowns, or when others of us were conducting field research in our mother tongues? Was Amélie's research in Saudi Arabia more authentic among Saudi nationals conducted in Arabic than her work in Dubai among French residents conducted in French, for example? And what kind of participant observation were we conducting if we did not even know how to map existing categories of residency and space onto the conversations and interactions we had?

We revisit and unpack some of our early ethnographic moments in chapter 1, through first-person field reflections that highlight the fraught experience of arrival, the ways it brings the complex reality of the place we call the field site in contact with the intellectual categories and representations of the field we carry with us as ethnographers. This allows us also to interrogate the ways of knowing human experience and subjectivity that we have naturalized through our academic disciplinary and political home sites, such as race, gender, and class.

Amélie began her fieldwork in Dubai with misconceptions that came not only from academic literature and media stereotypes but also from her previous experience of research in Riyadh. While one of her initial areas of focus was the relations between Western residents and national inhabitants in the professional world, the first moments of fieldwork led her to rethink the national/nonnational divide and what it meant in such a city. Her interactions with interviewees and the unease she felt in many situations incited her to question the specificities of Western positionalities in Dubai and their imbrication with whiteness, class, and gender. Continuing to elaborate on these themes in chapter 2, "How Western Residents in Riyadh and Dubai Produce and Challenge Exceptionalism," she discusses how exceptionalist discourses themselves shape Western subjectivities and positionalities in Riyadh and Dubai, based on two different research projects. Looking in particular at the category of Westerner, Amélie explores what the specific construction of this status—through various discourses and structural advantages on the job market—reveals about social hierarchies in terms of class, race, gender, and nationality and argues that such representations are central in forging distinctive Western subjectivities in both contexts.

In contrast to Amélie's feeling of strong ambivalence about her positionality as a white Western ethnographer, Neha, initially at least, felt "in her skin" for the first time in Dubai's South Asian neighborhoods, as she discusses in chapter 1. She felt this even as she had to learn new forms of gendered and classed relationality, particularly while interviewing elite Indian businessmen. But her belonging within the spaces occupied by the growing white expatriate population was difficult to negotiate, and the racism she experienced, even as an American, was unexpected. Feeling out of place in what she thought was a "home" neighborhood, and in place in the so-called nonplaces of New Dubai forced a reexamination of identity and her framings of Dubai as an Indian city. In chapter 3, "Anthropology and the Educational Encounter," Neha elaborates on these questions of difference, belonging, and immigration. Focusing on her experiences teaching, researching, and moving between different spaces in Education City, Doha, as it developed and changed during the period of her fieldwork, Neha thinks more specifically about how anthropological categories of difference have traveled with the migration of American institutions, disciplinary formations, and academics abroad. Paying particular attention to debates and contestations around gender "mixing," she argues that projects like Education City are not the exceptional spaces that most Western academics deem them to be, nor are they representative of the supposed failures of liberalism in so-called illiberal spaces. Instead, the way that the newly formed Hamad bin Khalifa University incorporated oppositional logics followed a long tradition in American higher education and showcased how a Qatari-American university can produce new imaginaries of pedagogy and decolonized knowledge production.

In his contribution to chapter 1, Ahmed describes how he initially experienced Dubai as an uneasy sci-fi "nonplace" even though he spoke Arabic, was in a self-described Muslim country, and could readily access Arab (both non-Emirati and Emirati) interlocutors. His interlocutors' mundane daily existence challenged his understanding of Dubai as a nonplace, and the presumptions of labor exploitation and repressive Gulf Arabs that accompany representations of Dubai as spectacular and dystopian. Reflecting on Henri Lefebvre's (2003) comment that all urbanism is in some way a class urbanism, Ahmed began to be drawn to the category of class as it plays out in journalistic and expert representations of the Gulf (Kanna 2011, 77–104). The trajectory of Ahmed's work, as is evident in chapter 4, "Class Struggle and De-exceptionalizing the Gulf," has been a clearer understanding of how urban discourses of "sci-fi" Dubai and the Gulf city as laboratory for urban formal experimentation are themselves not only exceptionalizing discourses but forms of class struggle, promoting imperial and capitalist class power in the Gulf. Attempting in chapter 4 to synthesize the postcolonial discursive critique with feminist Marxist conceptualizations of exploitation, Ahmed argues that a class struggle perspective both moves us beyond victimization discourses of Gulf labor and highlights global patterns of capitalist accumulation. Ahmed's chapter, like all of ours, utilizes particular postcolonial perspectives combined with class, race, and gender analysis to show not only how *unexceptional* the Gulf is but also how the Gulf can be a particularly generative site for ethnographic theory.

In the book's conclusion, we explore the question of what decolonized ethnography and academia can look like. While our aim with this project was to move the Arabian Peninsula beyond exception in our research framings and representations, we are invested in a broader strategy of bringing the region to the center of ethnographic theory and academic inquiry. Such a move would help reorient the current US-dominated imperial narratives and Eurocentric histories that still underpin anthropology and the university at large. De-exceptionalizing the Arabian Peninsula, therefore, also means placing decolonized knowledge from and about the region at the center of inquiry into the "global."

Notes

1. The sociological work that Amélie conducts as a scholar based in France is often considered as anthropology in the United States. Sociology in France is mostly qualitative, and ethnography is one of the most widespread methods among sociologists. Besides this, the postcolonial, feminist anthropology on the Middle East (mainly anglophone) has been one of the main inspirations of Amélie's work.

2. Jocelyn Sage Mitchell, "Why did Qatar just change its residency law?," *Washington Post*, August 9 2017, https://www.washingtonpost.com/news/monkey-cage/wp/2017/08/09/why-did-qatar-just-change-its-residency-laws/?utm_term=.0733e17128b6.

3. See Christina Lamb, "Under siege in the gilded cage of Qatar," *The Sunday Times*, June 11, 2017, https://www.thetimes.co.uk/article/what-is-life-like-during-qatar-blockade-6jljvhthq and Raymond Barrett, "Why Qatar Is in the Naughty Corner," *New York Times*, June 6, 2017, https://www.nytimes.com/2017/06/06/opinion/qatar-saudi-arabia-iran-trump.html.

4. See also "Game of Thrones a-la-Gulf: Saudi Royal Said to Be Calling to Family Members to Replace King," *RT*, September 24, 2015, https://www.rt.com/news/316348-saudi-royals-letter-replace-king/.

5. See, for example, Davis 2006; Malik 2009; and Badger, Cafiero, and Foreign Policy in Focus 2014, among many others.

6. See Gardner 2010; K. Leonard 2003; and Longva 1997 for discussions about difficulty accessing GCC countries as field researchers.

7. There are, however, academics and researchers who have been fired or arrested for their speech and activities. In the UAE, Matthew Hedges, a PhD student from the UK, was sentenced to life in prison and then pardoned in 2018, on the accusation that his research was actually spying. An Emirati professor of economics, Nasser bin Ghaith, is serving a ten-year sentence for his political activism, charged with "insulting" the UAE. Since the beginning of the rift with Qatar, censorship of news media has increased, as well as surveillance of online speech.

8. In France, for instance, the Gulf had been marginal in the field of Middle East studies until the 2000s. French Middle East studies, instead, focused more often on regions where France has had a colonial presence and where the French state has continued to try to maintain its influence through cultural and research centers. Since the 2000s, Gulf states have become more and more attractive clients for French industries, from armaments to transportation, and diplomatic relations have been reinforced. In the Peninsula, the French research center that used to be in Sanaa has been relocated to Kuwait as a consequence of the war in Yemen.

Chapter 1

Space, Mobility, and Shifting Identities in the Constitution of the "Field"

Neha Vora, Ahmed Kanna, Amélie Le Renard

In this chapter, we juxtapose previously unexplored experiences from our field diaries to highlight our shifting and contingent subject positions as we moved through urban spaces in the Arabian Peninsula and interacted with various interlocutors during our dissertation research. Reflecting back on these experiences after a combined three decades of research in Dubai, Doha, and Riyadh, we can see that we were unable to comprehend our relationship to our field sites and their inhabitants within the existing vocabularies of geography, identity, power, and belonging on the region, as well as more broadly within disciplinary and interdisciplinary literature on migration, transnationalism, and urbanism—vocabularies that we had naturalized prior to arrival. We present this conversational and reflexive piece as a call to develop more nuanced, relational, and grounded understandings of Gulf cities as ethnographic field sites, especially in relation to identity, labor, migration, diaspora, place, and belonging. How do we understand the boundaries of the groups that we study, for example, and the neighborhoods, mosques, high-rises, commercial centers, and public spaces that constitute their sense of home? Is our map of the "field" the same as their map of the city? How does our differential access and experience of urban space shape our interactions with our interlocutors, and thus the knowledge that we produce? Beginning to answer these difficult questions through a closer look at three very different research experiences—focusing on the seemingly highly stratified cities of Dubai, Doha, and Riyadh—can hopefully provide insights into designing and conducting urban fieldwork in other parts of the world as well. In so doing we also hope to highlight how prevalent ideas about identity in North American and European societies, which have heavily influenced postcolonial and postmodern anthropological attempts to be more inclusive and attentive to subject position, are also forms of baggage that academics (including those who occupy minoritized positions at "home") bring to the field.

We turn our critical gaze to our early field notes, those we did not originally consider data precisely because they exceeded the analytical categories through which we understood our research at the time. We examine our experiences of developing a research trajectory, arriving in and circumscribing our field, and navigating forms of discrimination, privilege, recognition, and misrecognition in relation to the spaces we occupied—in order to highlight how subjectivities in the Gulf are overlapping, sometimes contradictory, and contingent on geographical location, interactions with other urban residents (including scholars and journalists), and a range of other factors. In particular, we draw in this chapter on feminist and postcolonial traditions of reflexive ethnography that have deconstructed the figure of the social scientist as a neutral and unmarked observer (see, for example, Abu-Lughod 2013; Haraway 1988; Mankekar 1999). We borrow especially from Kirin Narayan's (1993) reflections on her role in the field and the academy, examining what it means to be "halfie" anthropologists: those in between modes of (unmarked) academic authority and (marked) "native" authenticity in and out of the Gulf, as well as precariously yet powerfully Western.

Two of us (Ahmed and Neha), having grown up as children of immigrants, learned rather quickly that the question "Where are you from?" was not innocent. It indicated that our racially marked bodies—one Iraqi American, the other Indian American—were decidedly foreign, inferior, and at times even suspect. These normalizations of belonging and identity followed us into the spaces of American academia, where the dominant categories in anthropology—as well as modes of marginalization in the discipline—are still structured in large part by race, heteronormative gender and kinship, class, and geographic location (Brodkin, Morgan, and Hutchinson 2011; Navarro, Williams, and Ahmad 2013). Experiences of marginalization in and out of academia began to shape our research trajectories. In addition, our political and scholarly stakes around identity intensified as we experienced and witnessed re-racializations after 9/11 (see Maira 2009; Puar 2007). Unsurprisingly, then, both of us chose field sites that we connected with racial/ethnic sameness and with transnational diasporic imaginaries. What is surprising, however, is that our original field site was the same: Dubai, a cosmopolitan city on the Arabian Peninsula that is Arab and South Asian simultaneously. The monographs that resulted from this fieldwork clearly echo one another, and yet surprisingly do not intersect as much as one might expect given the theoretical, temporal, and disciplinary framings of our research questions and methods (Kanna 2011; Vora 2013a). Neha went on to conduct intensive field research in Doha within university spaces and explores here how she had to address and undo old expectations as well as attend to new questions of authority, identity, and in-betweenness. Our third author, Amélie, presents a different experience, as a white researcher trained to be a European specialist of the "Arab world." Her long stays in the Saudi capital of Riyadh for her first field project led her to question her own positionality; as she explores below, this questioning informed her development of a new research agenda on "Western" residents in Dubai, which challenged her to confront the blurred boundaries of this privileged status.

The accounts we each present below from a combination of our memories leading up to fieldwork and quoted and summarized from our field notes showcase our divergent expectations of urban life in the Gulf and of our field experiences. We present them in our separate voices to emphasize just how much the cities that were overdetermined for us before we went to the field in the early to mid 2000s, through spectacular representations and a paucity of ethnographic literature, could still be experienced so differently.

How and why did our experiences of our field sites diverge so much from the literature that existed then? How did our different social statuses and positions influence these experiences? Which spaces and interlocutors did one of us have access to and not the others? How did our performances of identity shift as we moved through these cities and engaged different people? And what about our interactions with other Westerners, particularly white Westerners and fellow academics? The answers to these questions reveal a great deal about understandings of identity and space that we brought with us as migrating academics, and how daily life encounters informed and challenged these understandings.

In the Gulf, the question "Where are you from?" is not loaded in the same way it is in the United States or France. With populations that are up to 90 percent nonnational, almost everyone is a foreigner, and Arab and South Asian diasporas in particular are ubiquitous and historically entrenched. Despite being in a city, Dubai, where people looked like us, shared ethnoreligious backgrounds, and spoke our mother tongues, Ahmed and Neha still had to tackle negotiations of identity and place, familiarity and strangeness, several times a day. Meanwhile, Amélie faced this question regularly in Riyadh, which contrasted with her experience in France, where, as a white person, she never has to answer questions about her national/racial identity. As we moved through ever-changing neighborhoods and interacted with various residents, including our interlocutors in all of our field sites, we found that our lives constantly tacked between supposed insider and outsider in ways that were not contained by our learned or lived academic and home country understandings of these categories and who occupies them, nor by the everyday vocabularies of belonging and exclusion that supposedly define the Gulf, wherein one is either an "expat," "migrant," or "local," as we explore below. For us, field research in the Gulf—particularly the slippages that we experienced between various identities and spaces—undermined the naturalized ways that residency and politics there were presented to us before we arrived, and continue to be reproduced in academic and popular writing. Comparing our vastly different yet overlapping understandings of sociality, power, and space in Doha, Dubai, and Riyadh, we realized how our personal experiences were a fruitful site for the critical analysis of two key areas: first, of Gulf migration and its analytical categories, and second (and related to this), of the process of the anthropological reproduction of insider/outsider, native/foreign, strange/familiar, West/non-West, liberal/nonliberal, and related binaries (see also Ahmad 2017).

As researchers of the region, we present this conversational piece, then, as a way to encourage our readers to explore more fully how we all participate in producing our field sites before we even enter them, and to acknowledge and begin to undo our complicities in producing structures of power, belonging, and nonbelonging as we conduct and circulate scholarly research. We also are invested in this reflection in exploring new and productive critiques of identity-based politics, even as our academic and political stakes continue to invest, to varying degrees, in the importance of subject position and reflexivity as means for articulating and theorizing belonging and exclusion.

In what follows, we present urban fieldwork in the Gulf from three different angles that complement each other. Our narratives foreground the process of developing a critical sensibility in relation to dominant and often unconscious representations of Dubai; the relationship between mobility in different parts of Dubai and Doha and forms of comfort, authority, and identity politics; and the simultaneous deconstruction of "Western" stereotypes of Riyadh and Dubai and problematization of Western resident identities and positionalities. What unites our stories is how they trace and highlight a trajectory in which increasingly deep and informed participant observation and ethnographic engagement with Gulf cities and those who inhabit them bring to the fore unconscious assumptions about urban space and residency in the region. These assumptions are, in turn, critically positioned in relation to newer knowledge and subsequently are either overcome or unpacked and developed into different, more nuanced representations. What emerges from our narratives in conversation is, in short, a process by which empirical data, through the practice of reflexive and collaborative ethnography, yield more sophisticated theory.

Since we began our graduate careers, there has been a sharp increase in qualitative scholarship about the high levels of labor migration to the Arabian Peninsula, particularly to Dubai and Doha, cities that have aggressively pursued economic diversification and "post-oil" development initiatives in order to craft themselves as global cities and regional business and tourism hubs. This scholarship, some of which we introduced in the previous chapter, has been especially focused on highlighting the migration experiences and working conditions of low-wage construction workers from South and Southeast Asia, many of whom live in residence camps at the edges of the city, often in contrast to the luxury developments and spectacles of wealth that define the growing skylines of many of the Peninsula's cities, which are enjoyed by citizens, commonly referred to as "locals." "Gulf migration" has in many ways become synonymous with the worst form of labor exploitation in today's globalized economy, and instantaneously conjures up the now ubiquitous image of the Indian or Nepali man in blue coveralls seeking a moment of respite from the searing desert sun. Such a supposedly exceptional regime of labor exploitation is seemingly a direct result of the rigid hierarchical structure of Gulf residency. This structure has come to be defined as ethnocracy, following the work of Ahn Nga Longva (1997, 2005), which highlights how noncitizens are excluded from almost all aspects of national identity and the social welfare benefits of oil wealth, as well as to the kafala system of migrant governance that appears to be unique to the region.[1]

However, as cities like Dubai, Doha, and Riyadh have grown both during and after the discovery of oil and state formation, they have required not only low-wage labor but also professional expertise—thus producing a parallel managerial class, commonly referred to as expatriates. This "expat" is often represented in popular media (both local and international), in Gulf advertisements for luxury housing and shopping developments, and in the narratives of Gulf residents themselves as a wealthy, white, cosmopolitan subject, usually from Europe or North America, even though Gulf companies recruit professionals from around the world to fill high-level positions. It is commonly understood that Gulf residents fall into one of three categories: citizen, expatriate, or migrant laborer. These categories tend to not only homogenize nationals and their supposed elite status (which not all nationals experience) but also produce normative understandings of migration in which one group (migrant laborers) is presumed to be uniformly exploited, subaltern, unskilled, and from the Global South, while the other (expatriates) marks white, mobile professionals from the Global North (Kanna 2011; Vora 2013a, 2014b).

The Gulf expat remains relatively understudied and undertheorized as an important symbolic, historical, and material category of foreign residency. We explore the production of the expat as a symbolic field in which imperial histories, concepts of race, neoliberal urban development, and nationalism intersect—and most importantly, how this field includes and is produced by scholars and other knowledge workers in and of the Gulf. Migrant middle classes and elites participate in transnational regimes of race, class, gender, and patronage that are not unique to the Gulf region. And they have been historical actors in reproducing labor practices from around the Indian Ocean, within Europe and North America, and within the Arabian Peninsula.[2] By examining the role of expats as both migrant laborers and participants in labor exploitation and class hierarchy, we encourage an approach to labor and migration in the Gulf that highlights the region's connection to global networks rather than one that reproduces tropes of its supposed exceptionalism (see also Hanieh 2011). In addition, we place the academic researcher within the categories of labor and residency that exist within the

Arabian Peninsula's urban spaces, asking how the practice of research and the embodied subjectivity of the researcher shape and are shaped by the ever-changing modes of identification, difference, belonging, and mobility on the ground.

Sci-fi Dubai: Ahmed's First Field Encounters as an Iraqi American Anthropologist

Although I spent part of my childhood in Kuwait, I didn't become interested in the Gulf region until the early 2000s when, working with my academic advisor, a prominent scholar in the tradition of the Frankfurt School, I became drawn to urbanism and the built environment as anthropological questions. At the time, Dubai seemed like an ideal place to pursue such a project, as the city was rapidly transitioning into a seemingly new and globalized entity. My curiosity was also related to my family's national identity and migration experience. In 1980, my family emigrated from our native Iraq to Kuwait. Even though Kuwait had a large Iraqi population (Iraqis would leave en masse during and after the 1991 Gulf War), I grew up with a sense that my Iraqiness was distinct from Gulf Arab culture. I was taught that "we" were from the "authentic" Arab world, one of ancient civilizations. Mesopotamia, I was told, invented cities, writing, and legal codes. From an Iraqi nationalist perspective, Kuwait and the rest of the Gulf were nonplaces: instant cities with no history and fast-food cultures built by the petrodollars of a nouveau riche. This was an ironic claim, as I would learn years later, given that Iraq was stereotyped in the same ways when it was experiencing its first postindependence oil development in the late 1950s and 1960s. This sense of Iraqi superiority intensified during and after 1991, despite the fact that many Iraqis, including my family, were against the invasion of Kuwait. Mutual hostility was only exacerbated by the Kuwaiti state's embrace of US imperialism in the region, which devastated Iraq's economy and society during the same period. This complex skein of nationalist ideology, collective memory, and historical events contributed significantly both to my curiosity about the Gulf and to my ready acceptance of the tropes that circulated about it in popular media and scholarly literature.

My academic preparation prior to fieldwork was a corrective to these stereotypes, but an incomplete one. The literature I explored prior to fieldwork proposed a way of looking at questions of experience and the built environ-ment that most of the anthropological literature on cities, and certainly the regional literature on the Gulf, was missing: a serious engagement *both* with architecture and urban design, and with the politics and social processes shaping what gets built and for whom. While this work inspired new ways of approaching urban form, I also began to carry these texts as more unwieldy baggage: I wanted to read Dubai as a kind of oneiric space, like Benjamin's (2002) Paris Arcades or Kracauer's (1995) hotel lobby. There is much in my early field notes from 2002 to 2004 where I write about Dubai as a weird dreamscape or sci-fi movie set. This approach reflected what was becom-ing a standardized repertoire of writing on Gulf cities as hyperbolic spaces of "supermodernity" and the worst aspects of globalization. I tended, for example, to view working-class migrants, whether construction workers or domestic laborers or others, as a homogeneously oppressed mass laboring under a wealthy Emirati national population. What I was unable to see at the time was that my early field notes also reveal how the workaday lives of most of my Arab interlocutors, whether foreign residents or UAE citizens, were generally distant and disconnected from these assumptions about labor, urbanism, and stark citizen/migrant dichotomy.[3] If my interlocutors did discuss "sci-fi" Dubai, it was to subject it to ironic humor or ambivalent readings of modernity. To my exceptionalizing discourses of "Dubai, Inc." and "dreamscape Dubai," they offered de-exceptionalizing points of view in which the city emerged as a product of ordinary, even uninteresting, pro-cesses of technopolitics, geopolitics, and cultural politics—processes that were similar to those occurring in more "authentic" Middle Eastern cities at the time (Bogaert 2018; Deeb and Harb 2013; Fawaz 2009, 2014; Hourani and Kanna 2014).

One day in mid-December 2003, for example, I noted in my field diary that it was impossible to write field notes because the media was exploding with news that US marines had found Saddam Hussein hiding out in a hole in rural Iraq. The Iraqi community of Dubai, with which I was by then in-timately connected, was dumbfounded. Most seemed, like me, overwhelmed and unable to articulate what exactly this event portended. The general feel-ing was that this would augur something even darker or more chaotic than the years of wars and sanctions from 1980 to 2003. Global media—Al Jazeera, Alarabiyya, BBC World Service, CNN International—and the Internet formed an infrastructural condition of possibility around which Dubai's Iraqi community came together to follow news of their home country and to try to interpret the direction of events. The presence of these media and the structures of their reception, in turn, were conditioned by the spatial politics of Dubai, in which the city was rising to the top of various lists of global cities, a global that was defined by spectacular urban design, neoliberal consumerism and advertising, and access to state-of-the-art communications and technology.

The media images and news stories from Iraq kept flooding in. News of bombings arrived seemingly every day and were constantly repeated throughout the twenty-four-hour media cycle. A pall of hopelessness descended on the Iraqi community. Then came the peaks of brutality that set themselves off from the grisly norm, events such as Abu Ghraib and Fallujah. Ali, an Iraqi in his thirties from a middle-class family who had immigrated to Dubai in the aftermath of the US invasion, shared his views with me as we drove together during Ramadan (which fell in late fall that year). Saddam Hussein, he said, was a *thalim* (tyrant), but the United States has come for nothing but its own interests: friends don't come on the backs of tanks (*ala thahr al dabbabat*). I asked him how his life has changed since he came to Dubai. "Are you happy?" I asked Ali. "You don't really have any other choice," he said matter of factly. Dubai, for Ali, was neither spectacular nor insane, but blasé, a practical place where he could escape from an impossible situation in Iraq through seemingly interminable hard work.

Muhammad, another Iraqi with a similar social background and emigration story, echoed Ali when he compared Iraq to the UAE: "If you look at the Emirati rulers, they are corrupt. Corrupt as anyone. But they also let you live your life. You're free to have a job and make your money and they leave you alone. They say, 'I have my money; here, have yours, and let's live together.'" A group of Emirati young men with whom I was hanging out at a Ramadan *iftar* some time later said something similar to me about the ordinariness of daily life. While these Emiratis were not bad off by any means—they had government jobs and were economically stable—the spectacular Dubai of star architecture and glittering malls was of no interest to them. They avoided such spaces because they felt excluded from them, preferring instead the homes of compatriots, drives in the desert, and cafés in less famous and flashy parts of the city.

Khaled, a British Egyptian social scientist based in Dubai, shared Muhammad's focus on Arab government corruption over many conversations we had during my fieldwork. He would often turn his experiences growing up in Egypt and the UAE dealing with *al-nithaam* (the bureaucracy)—along with his experiences of racism in Britain—into hysterically funny jokes. *Ashab as-sumuww wa-l fakhama, tfoo alaikum*! was a favorite saying of his, which he borrowed from a long history of Arab political humor, turning a conventional address of respect to Arab rulers into "Honored and eminent dignitaries, I spit on you!" Though neither of us loved malls, we often met at a popular one over coffee because of its convenience. During one of these meetings he said, contemptuously, waving to our surroundings, "the Khaleejis [Gulf Arabs], I can't get over how they turned all that money into this." While it would be tempting to interpret Khaled as expressing a conventional Arab snobbery toward the Gulf, like the one I had grown up with, Khaled was often even more scathing about non-Gulf Arab countries. Instead, he situated his critique of both Gulf and non-Gulf Arab power relations, along with the flaws of the British society in which he grew up, in his left-wing politics and universalist Enlightenment values.

Yusuf, another Iraqi immigrant, who, like his brother Ali (mentioned earlier), made a downward class transition from middle-class professional to service worker in immigrating to the UAE, took up a main theme of discussions on Dubai in the twenty-first century. From the media to everyday conversations, especially among immigrant Arabs, the rise of Dubai as a leader of the Arab world, replacing traditional cultural and political capitals such as Baghdad, Beirut, and Cairo, was a major topic. Yusuf said that he does not believe that Dubai, or the Gulf, represents *tatawwur* (progress). Tatawwur must come from *thihn al-insan*, from "inside," or from *thaat al-insan*, the human being's essence. In other words, it must be authentic and come from within the people rather than from without. It cannot be imposed. He meant both the Gulf and Iraq: in the case of the former, what he saw as the Gulf's imitation of Western modernity; in the case of the latter, the US project to "bring democracy" on the backs of tanks. As Arabs, he said, we seem to be stuck between *al-sinaa'a* (manufacturing—i.e., creative, autonomous production) and *al-tasannu'* (the mere importation of the methods of industry, the imitation of the techniques of foreigners). "When I manufacture a certain object," he said in Arabic, "I have a choice. I can either direct it [*aqud-ha*], or I can allow it to direct me [*akhalleeha tqudni*]." Al-sinaa'a is when you control your own creations. Al-tasannu' is when you let your own creations control you. Iraq and the UAE became indistinguishable in this comment, the case of occupied neocolony and capitalist so-called dreamland blending into one condition of ambivalent or even negative modernity.

Rereading my earliest field notes over a decade after the fact is striking in the ways my position as a field worker was distantiated and focused on the surface qualities of urban experiences in Dubai despite daily interactions that belied this representation. I do not want to minimize the significance of the surface qualities of Dubai's urban form. For my Emirati interlocutors, especially, as well as for many of my non-Emirati Arab interlocutors, Dubai's architecture was a symbol of modernity, or, at least, provided an opportunity to reflect on this condition. This being said, however, the stark contrast between everyday people's generally unexceptional experiences of Dubai's urbanity and the more exceptionalizing discourses of experts such as the architects whom I had also been interviewing for my research, who tended to talk about Dubai as an "experiment" in urban formalism, was jarring. This contrast invites a deeper questioning of the process by which understandings of the very category of the city get produced, circulate, and become common sense. For ethnographers this has interesting implications. If arrival as a literary device central to anthropological writing is based on an assumed break between the "home" of the anthropologist and that of the subjects of anthropological writing, as we explored in the introduction, and if the *locus classicus* of anthropological knowledge is the isolated village or island, are tropes of "globality" and "urbanism," then, truly correctives to these conventional anthropological imagined geographies? Or do the latter simply map onto, and reinforce, romantic anthropological constructions of the cultural other? Can the "global" or the "urban" truly help us rethink the motifs of "outsider" and "insider" so central to the concept of the anthropological field? As, I believe, this section and the next ones show, a relational and reflexive concept of identity may be more helpful in de-exceptionalizing the Gulf city as a field site.

Unimagining Community: Neha's Experiences of Familiarity and Discomfort

Unlike Ahmed, I came to Dubai with the expectation that I was arriving not in a dreamscape but in a more real "real" against which to situate my life experiences and political stakes, a middle-ground city between India and the United States and a diasporic community that I already felt connected to. I presumed Dubai would be more authentically Indian because it was close to the subcontinent, because people traveled back and forth more often and with greater ease, because there were no paths to citizenship and assimilation, and mostly, because there were just so many more of "us" there. This expectation of Dubai, like my coauthors', came out of my own academic and personal experiences before fieldwork.

In college, through encounters with identity politics, women's studies, and ethnic studies, I came to better understand my experiences growing up nonwhite in the United States, as well as how they were mediated by class, gender, and the cultural politics of Indian diasporic communities. In graduate school I was introduced by my advisors to postcolonial theory and transnational feminism—through reading Gayatri Spivak, Inderpal Grewal and Caren Kaplan, Aihwa Ong, and Chandra Mohanty, I began to de-domesticate my understandings of diaspora and racialization. Since the literature on South Asian diaspora was so heavily weighted toward North America and the United Kingdom, I decided to focus on South Asian communities in a non-Western or non–Global North location for my research.

In the burgeoning media coverage of Dubai that coincided with my lead-up to fieldwork, I noticed that there was little reference to Dubai's large South Asian population. At that time, the media and academic attention to labor exploitation and human rights in the region was not as heightened as it is today. If mentioned at all in historical or anthropological accounts of the Gulf, South Asians were afforded a passing reference, either to their privileged positions as merchants within the British Raj or to contemporary migrant labor circuits that were central to Dubai's construction boom. However, Indian Ocean historiographies (especially of merchants) and emerging urban anthropology in Gulf cities gave me some idea of deeper cultural impacts that Indians and other South Asians might be having on these places where they were supposedly temporary, and the impacts that the Gulf might be having on identity and on global understandings of India and Indianness (Al Sayegh 1998; Das Gupta 2004; K. Leonard 2003; Lombard and Aubin 2000; Osella and Osella 2006). I was interested in constituting my field through the narratives and traces of Indianness that I found in this literature. However, I also presumed that the vocabulary through which GCC structures of citizenship, migration, and governance were presented in the limited work on the region at that time (in comparison with other parts of the Middle East) coincided with entirely different daily existences than my own: Indians were, I believed, not permanent, without rights, and therefore not bicultural.

I had decided at first to focus my research on older trade diasporas, in order to center transnational connections and the history of Indians in Dubai, specifically through gold merchants and their memories of pre-oil Dubai. Every morning for the first few months of fieldwork in 2006, I walked from my apartment, which was on the edge of Dubai's crowded Bur Dubai neighborhood, to the Dubai Creek, where I took an *abra* (water taxi) into the Gold Souk area. Here I would begin field research for the day, watching wholesale and retail trade, interviewing gold merchants and shop workers, and noting consumption patterns. In the early afternoons I would make my way back across the Creek, usually stopping to grab a quick lunch in one of Bur Dubai's *dosa* shops, and to buy groceries from either an Indian store like Choitram's or the more expat Spinney's. I would spend the rest of my afternoon lingering in a shopping mall to get out of the heat, or stop at an Internet café to check emails and write field notes before heading back home. My early ethnographic map did not extend into the Western expatriate "edges" that I traversed and occupied as part of my daily life, and my field notes do not include much detail about those places and activities. I almost solely focused on what I considered the authentic—that is, Indian—parts of Dubai, and my notes became increasingly full of concerns about what I was not finding in them. As I discuss in a chapter of the book based on this fieldwork, for example, my research among merchants was particularly frustrating: their narratives felt too scripted, and I had trouble analyzing them and moving forward with new research questions (Vora 2013a).

What I didn't have the capacity to understand at the time was how much I was unable to connect with many of the people I encountered in early fieldwork. The mostly male spaces of the souks were taking a daily toll on me, as were the ways that gender and age differences played out in my conversations with merchants—they were older, were very wealthy, openly made inappropriate comments about my appearance, and in retrospect, regularly employed a paternalistic form of sexual harassment. The very things that provided me with the access that I had to these "big men"—my age, my South Asianness, and my gender—were also what made fieldwork lonely, stressful, and challenging.

My embodied awareness of being a woman in mostly male space extended into my encounters with the service workers, taxi drivers, and other (primarily working class) South Asian men I interacted with regularly. However, in these encounters, my middle-class and Western status, as well as the fact that I was usually engaging them as a customer, meant that their precarity—classed, raced, and passport-based—came into further relief when having to interact with women in a country where discourses of women's protection were used to police "bachelor" mobility and access to space. I dreaded these encounters because they required, on both of our parts, a very controlled and uncomfortable performativity, one that was laden with heterosocial tension. Despite these challenges, I also felt closer to my "Indianness" than I ever had in my life, and I began to practice the consumer citizenship that I describe in my book (Vora 2013a). I adopted a field uniform of *kurta* and jeans, ate in Indian restaurants, watched Bollywood movies, shopped at South Asian grocery stores, and practiced my rapidly improving Hindi as often as I could. For the first time in my life, I could go days without thinking about my brown skin, a racial comfort that I found so unfamiliar that it bordered on painful.

A couple months into my fieldwork, I began to slip in my daily routine, taking cabs out to Ahmed's sci-fi "New Dubai" to wander around the fancy shopping malls and hotels, spending money I didn't have on expensive lunches or lazing away my time reading a novel in a nice hotel lobby. In New Dubai I was a different person. I traded my *kurta* and jeans for sundresses and heels, I spoke English, and I consumed Western brands and products. As I guiltily noted one afternoon in my diary about a week into doing "nothing," I felt comfortable there, but I couldn't then articulate why I wanted to escape from the neighborhoods that I considered my home spaces in the city. I was so invested in ideas of authenticity around Indianness that I did not give appropriate attention to the ways that I felt out of place in old Dubai, and what feeling in place and out of place simultaneously could tell me about both my field site and my research project.

At first I took my discomfort in old Dubai as a glaring reminder of how growing up American made me more disconnected from my "culture" than my interlocutors were. This was a comment that many people I interviewed rehearsed about "Non-Resident Indians" (NRIs) in the West, so it was not that far-fetched. Feeling that I was not adequately insider enough prevented me first from acknowledging and later from criticizing the classed, ethnic, religious, and gendered valences of Indian diasporic community formations in Dubai and the erasures and violences they enacted. Feeling that I was an insider, on the other hand, was preventing me from truly hearing my interlocutors' experiences, for I expected too much for them to be like me, and I initially uncritically tried to understand them through scripts of what I already knew firsthand and through previous research: Western diasporic cultural and generational conflict narratives, and Asian American stories of immigration as permanent settlement away from and nostalgia for the "homeland." It was only in reflecting back on what I then thought were my own failures to belong that I was able to see that my interlocutors were meaningfully *different* from me in ways that were just as important as how they were similar, and that without acknowledging those differences, my scholarship could not adequately represent their everyday lives.

Eventually, I decided not to look for historical traces of Indianness in the souks but to talk to a whole range of Indians about their lives in Dubai in relation to migration, work, family, and community. I needed to unpack my identity baggage in order to arrive at a new understanding of my field. This unpacking also required addressing my experiences in New Dubai as just as ethnographically important as my experiences in old Dubai. In my search for "roots" in old Dubai, I neglected my own Western complicity in the projects of Brand Dubai. I practiced my consumer citizenship not only as an Indian but also as a privileged Western subject who could enter into the luxury spaces of Dubai's commercial and tourism boom without suspicion; and I could, even on a graduate student salary, consume some of the lifestyle and products offered in these spaces. In addition, shopping malls were feminine spaces, in contrast to the masculine street life of the Dubai Creek area. They provided, therefore, not only middle-class comfort but also gendered safety. I came to see over my time in Dubai that I occupied different subject positions and embodied performances (sartorial, linguistic, gendered, raced, classed) as I moved through various parts of the city. This helped me to better understand the heterogeneity of various migrant groups, and Indians especially, who were so omnipresent that it was impossible to classify them wholesale as "migrant laborers."

New Dubai, however, had its own set of discomforts and exclusions that I had to navigate. As Amélie explores in greater detail below, the expat is a category that encompasses a number of nationalities and is itself not easily bounded even as it is marked by white privilege, legacies of white colonial pleasure/leisure, and Western *habitus* (Kanna 2014; Le Renard 2019a; Walsh 2006). The built environments of Dubai, along with ethnoracial understandings of who belongs in which spaces, enabled forms of segregation and self-segregation, allowing for illiberal comforts of white space that ironically could not be found as readily in Euro-American countries. This means that racism and essentialized assumptions about different nationalities are normalized into the fabric of the city. I remember in the first few days of living in Dubai being in line at Spinney's and listening to two white British men in front of me have a racist conversation about all of the reasons why Indians were bad coworkers; they either assumed I didn't speak English, didn't see me, or didn't care. I had a white professor at a university in the UAE ask me, with no qualms, whether there is something genetically different about Indians that makes the construction workers so "small." And I have experienced going to American parties and having no one socialize with me because I was not white, or perhaps presumed to be not American. A ubiquitous joke between my white friends and me, which I think was meant to defuse tension as well as distance us from Dubai's racial hierarchies, was whether people wonder if I am their maid when we go out in public together. In addition to racial discrimination, the shopping malls and hotels in New Dubai also produced anxieties around wealth, leading to what I always felt were false performances of fully belonging in those spaces.

My feelings of belonging and not belonging in Dubai could be read as derivative of the typical Western "bicultural" diasporic subject. However, my understandings and experiences of both my South Asian background and my Americanness were not the same in Dubai or in Doha, the site of my next research project on American university branch campuses, as they are in the United States, and required a reimagining of how class, gender, race, and space informed my daily life as a foreign resident researcher, as well as the daily lives of my informants. Arriving in Doha, I expected a city very similar to Dubai, since it was similarly developing—and similarly exceptionalized in media descriptions as a site of either extreme Qatari wealth, on the one hand, or extreme migrant labor exploitation, on the other. As these migrants were primarily South Asian, I presumed I would find another "India West" with large Western expatriate-dominated areas akin to New Dubai. While Doha did indeed have older neighborhoods with South Asian residents, and newer growing pockets of luxury hotels and malls that catered to wealthy foreigners, the city had a much larger Arab immigrant population, without the deep connections to the subcontinent that Dubai had, both historically and during my fieldwork. In addition, the shopping mall and consumer culture of Dubai was markedly different from Doha's emphasis on museums, art, and heritage. I found myself having to learn a new city, and while many of the racial and class dynamics of the UAE were similar in Qatar, they were also not the same. My non-Muslimness, something that barely affected my daily life in Dubai, was something I had to navigate in Doha, especially as I saw shifting norms of gender surveillance and segregation over the years of my research. Within American campuses, I was read mostly as Western by my students, including my Qatari students, an experience I had not had in my few guest appearances in UAE classrooms. Meanwhile, I had to contend with both Gulf- and US-based hierarchies of racialization when it came to fitting in among many of the white North American faculty members. These differences and similarities, and the way they also point to questions of embodied expertise and authority (which we return to briefly below), showcase the need to not only de-exceptionalize Gulf cities but also disaggregate "the Gulf" as a homogenous field space, which Amélie continues to explore in her account.

Navigating Whiteness: Amélie's Journey from Riyadh to Dubai

During my repeated stays in Riyadh, between 2005 and 2012, in order to complete my PhD on Saudi women's lifestyles and transforming femininity norms, I frequented two main types of spaces (outside of King Faisal research center, where I was hosted as an invited researcher): women-only spaces, where I spent most of my time; and the diplomatic quarter (DQ), where I rented a flat that belonged to the French embassy.[4] In women-only spaces, I met almost no white people. In Riyadh, most white Western residents were either men with high-ranking management jobs or so-called "accompanying wives", who were not allowed to work professionally, living in circumscribed, securitized spaces that were designed for them, such as gated communities (where Saudi nationals are not allowed to live). I did not have such status, and moved outside those spaces. I avoided spending time in the DQ and attended only one or two "embassy parties," as some Saudi friends called them. At these regular events organized by Western embassies, guests, who were mainly Western residents, including the minority migrating as singles and working in the military, as nurses, or as English teachers, could drink alcohol (forbidden in Saudi Arabia but tolerated inside the DQ) and meet each other. I fled such gatherings, though I realize now how interesting it would have been to analyze how these people negotiated belonging and relations in a context where various institutions imposed very strict categories and various segregations (see chapter 2). I felt uncomfortable, in general, with how the French people I met talked about Saudis, and with some of their behaviors, too. Limiting interactions permitted me to escape from complicated questions about power relations and my role there, questions I might not have been able to tackle at the time. I remained focused on my research and spent as much time as possible with young Saudi women, conducting an intensive ethnography.

Maybe because of these differences with most white Western residents, I experienced relatively flexible and shifting identifications in women-only spaces, where I mainly interacted with Saudi women. Some of them addressed me as a "Westerner," a word I often heard while doing fieldwork. A few years after the US wars on Iraq and Afghanistan, I was sometimes asked if I agreed with Bush's policy, as if I were a US citizen. I realized that, especially in Sahwist milieus,[5] speaking about Saudi women—or wanting to know more about them—was associated with Western, and especially US, imperialism; this encouraged me to pay attention to imperialism as a central aspect of contemporary debates about women's activities and rights.

Most women, however, did not project such images on me; my speaking Arabic, with an accent that sounded increasingly Saudi, helped me meet women from various backgrounds and make friendships. Navigating the city, I learned to change self-presentations depending on spaces and gatherings. For a long time, I thought this was an ethnographer's "trick," before realizing that this practice was very common among young urban Saudi women as well. One specific self-presentation and role I had to learn was how to react when faced with the authorities. Policemen or officers often interpreted my presence, as a woman navigating the city alone in taxis (a means of transportation considered lacking in prestige at that time), as weird, if not suspect. Little by little, I understood that when interacting with police officers, I had better throw my veil back on my shoulders, show my passport, and perform the French-that-does-not-even-speak-English. In other words, I realized that my passport protected me more than whatever I could say, and I had to conform to the stereotypes attached to my nationality—which says a lot about national/Western privilege, since such a strategy works only for specific nationalities.

My access to women-only spaces and gatherings, as well as my experiences and friendships with Saudi women, contrasted with many DQ French residents' discourses about Saudi society as "closed." After obtaining my PhD, I got interested in the self-segregated lifestyles Western residents adopted, their positions in professional local environments, and the stereotypes they developed about Saudi men and women. I began to question the category of "Westerner" in the Arabian Peninsula. This new research interest was unlikely given my training as a specialist of the "Arab world": the masters program I had pursued was actually named "Muslim world," and I had learned Arabic in Cairo, Damascus, and Paris. My desire to study Westerners in the Peninsula had several motives. First, in various contexts, I felt misunderstood when I spoke about my PhD research, which dealt with young Saudi women's mobile lifestyles and transformations in femininity norms (Le Renard 2014a). On any subject related to "women in Saudi Arabia," exceptionalist, Orientalist visions deeply influenced the possible reception of a presentation. I had the feeling that whatever I said, people would remember only the one element that verified their stereotypes. One of my aims when changing subjects was to address these stereotypes more directly, to leave no space for their reproduction. Second, I wanted to shed light on the transnational "connections" (Abu-Lughod 1991) that contributed to shaping norms of national professional femininity: national women's employment and the nationalization of jobs were two key points of the proclaimed economic reform in Saudi Arabia and some neighboring countries. US, British, and other European embassies supported such policies, and I wondered what role some Western residents may play in them. Third, such focus was also a way to question my position as a part-time resident in the Arabian Peninsula, what it meant to be white and Western there, and which power relations shaped my status.[6]

I arrived in Dubai for the first time in 2012 in order to deepen the questions raised by my research in Riyadh. My preconceptions were many: I thought that it would be easier to conduct research in Dubai than in Riyadh, that the Western/white people living in Dubai would have about the same characteristics as those living in Riyadh (i.e., mainly men on comfortable expatriate contracts and women on "dependent" visas), and that it would be possible and interesting to work on the interactions between Westerners and nationals as I had done in a multinational bank in Riyadh in 2011–2012 (see chapter 2). The first weeks of fieldwork led me to complexify my vision of Westerners.

After a first enthusiastic phase before my arrival—apparently, everybody knew somebody living in Dubai, so it was easy to find contacts that would help me—I realized once in Dubai that research in this city would not be easier than in Riyadh. The discourse on Riyadh's "closed" character, as with the one on Dubai's "openness"/"modernity," is stereotypical, obscuring more complex realities. While looking for a firm in which to conduct field research similar to that which I had conducted in Riyadh, I faced reluctance. On the one hand, many (white) people I met were not interested in social science or did not understand what I was researching. For instance, after I explained my research to a manager in the French Alliance (a center of French teaching but also a node of Francophone networking), hoping she would connect me to helpful persons, she told me I should prepare an advertising brochure on my project, and slipped out. On the other hand, many professionals, even high-ranking managers, expressed fear about the possible consequences, for themselves, of participating in my research and of giving me access to their firm or colleagues.

After several emails, the regional manager of an important local firm working in the field of luxury, a white British man, finally met me in a small meeting room close to the entrance door. He refused to answer all the questions about his work and the firm, while at the same time elaborating on his family life. He insisted that Dubai had fulfilled his wish to have a better family life: his wife had been able to stop working professionally thanks to his lucrative employment package. This strict division of work between spouses, shaping particular family forms and heteronormativity among upper-class Western residents, would later become an important part of my research (Le Renard 2019a, 2019b). Concluding our very short interview, the regional manager asked me to send the work-related questions by email for him to check the information with his higher-ups. He never answered my email. In Riyadh, most Saudi and European people I had met seemed not to care much, in general, about the legal/illegal, and several had invited me to their workplaces without precautions. In contrast, the white Western people I met in Dubai, especially those on local contracts, were preoccupied with their possible dismissal. Their status was both extremely advantageous, in terms of salaries, packages, and positions, compared with that of other employees, and more fragile than in Riyadh, where most white Western people benefited from expatriate contracts. In Dubai, the Western residents with high positions I met had adopted very costly, consumerist lifestyles, and some had developed anxiety about being fired, getting expelled from the country, and losing a lot of money. At other moments during these interviews, however, several praised Dubai's "security," underlining the comfort of living in a place where there was, apparently, no stealing and no aggression: a pacified social order. While this discourse revealed important elements of upper-class white Western positionalities in Dubai, the only way through which I was finally able to enter firms was to meet the owners rather than the high-ranking managers.

Another step in my fieldwork was to understand that Emiratis would be almost absent from my research. In Riyadh, I had realized at the end of my PhD research that my initial choice to focus exclusively on Saudi women reproduced both the national ideology of the state and, to some extent, an Orientalist search for authenticity—"real" Saudis, excluding the many residents who had been living in the country for decades without getting nationality. My response had been to problematize how gender norms and forms of distinction played a role in constructing the national/nonnational hierarchy in my academic work. In the media, when journalists called me to talk about "women in Saudi Arabia," I tried to include information about nonnational women. Such information was often considered off topic, as if "Saudi women" and "workers and maids" were on two different planets, and as if maids were not women living in Saudi Arabia. Even academic approaches to the Arabian Peninsula often treat the "nationals" and "migrants" as two separate subjects and fields. This is what led me to work on interactions between nonnational and national managers and employees in a multinational bank, after my PhD.

While I wanted to adopt a similar approach in Dubai, I realized that Emiratis were physically absent from most of the private sector workplace. To persist in searching for such interactions would be to reproduce, once again, a vision of authenticity according to which Emiratis were the only "real" inhabitants of Dubai. A few interviews at the beginning of my fieldwork helped me understand this bias: not meeting Emiratis sounded like a major source of frustration for some French women I met. This desire for authenticity and exoticism helped shape distinctive white subjectivities, as I discuss later in this book. Trips to Oman's touristic sites, where a fantasy of authenticity was performed and made accessible to visitors, may be interpreted as a way to ease the frustration of those who perceived Dubai as lacking exoticism (see also Coles and Walsh 2010).

As I decided to focus on interviewing various residents who held "Western" passports, I realized that the frontiers of Westernness were blurred, more obviously and massively than in Riyadh. I was facing a paradox. On the one hand, being white seemed to imply very specific conduct, which contrasted with what I had personally experienced in Riyadh. In the Saudi capital, Arabic was often the only language I had to communicate with people (even when it was not their mother tongue either). In Dubai, I mainly spoke English, and never Arabic. An intuition led me to anticipate that it would have sounded awkward for a white person. To some extent, I felt I had to conform to a certain stereotype of whiteness/Westernness/Frenchness, not only in front of the police, as I did in Riyadh, but also in many social interactions. It is difficult to know exactly what engendered such a feeling and whether it was just my own projection.[7] Some remarks addressed to me, however, were clear appreciations of my conduct in light of my status as a white person.

During my first stay, for example, some French interviewees commented on the fact that my hotel was in an area of the city (Deira) lacking prestige and connoted as "Indian" (a word used to designate people on a racialized basis, beyond the Indian nationality). Such remarks were part of the routine anti-Indian racism I observed among white/Western communities, already mentioned above by Neha. It also revealed that white people were supposed to navigate the city following certain maps. Deira was a place to go only occasionally: it was considered as more authentic and exotic than so-called artificial Dubai, built for well-off nonnational residents but backward, dirty, and far from "everything"—that is, far from the shopping malls, bars, and restaurants where most white people went out.

As my Dubai research went on, I felt increasingly uncomfortable in the milieus I studied, not well dressed enough, not feminine, and not able to "sell myself." Having grown up in a business-oriented family in a middle-sized city in France, I could have conformed with these norms more easily earlier in my life, but I had been taking another path for many years. I did not embody the right heteronormative, consumerist femininity. And everything seemed too expensive to me, since my permanent researcher's salary in France was much lower than most of my interviewees' salaries in Dubai.

As often, the unease was hard to experience but productive for my thinking. Networking techniques, and especially the performance of stereotypical professional Westernness, became one focus of my analysis. Many people I met had found their jobs once in Dubai, since having a Western passport allowed them to visit the Emirates on a free tourist visa.[8] To "sell them-selves" on Dubai's job market, they had worked on dress, superficial interac-tions, and casual joking for their self-presentations to conform to a certain model of professional Westernness—a model that was gendered, heteronor-mative, racialized, and classed. Embodying Brand Dubai implied specific performances of the self. In this game, the people who were white, fluent in English (with an American or British accent), and conformed to dominant gender norms were structurally advantaged. Those with middle- or upper-class backgrounds were advantaged too, but it was also common to meet Western people with working-class backgrounds, high salaries, and seem-ingly expensive branded clothes and accessories in these gatherings.

On the other hand, people with Western passports, all benefiting from certain structural advantages on the job market, nevertheless had diverse tra-jectories and contrasting statuses. Some had been raised in the region, while others had grown up in Europe or North America; only a minority were white. Beyond white people and whiteness, which have been the focus of most postcolonial approaches of expatriation (Fechter and Walsh 2010), complex processes of inclusion and exclusion shaped Dubai's Westerners. The concept of whiteness remains completely useful to analyze the advantages that con-struct the privileged status of white residents in Dubai. However, enlarging the focus helps us consider the complex racializations of nationality, and their co-construction with class and gender, on Dubai's job market and in vari-ous social interactions. In the last phase of my fieldwork, I chose to interview only people with French nationality in order to deepen my understanding of these dimensions. It meant interviewing both white professional "expa-triates" from the upper and upper-middle classes, often living in Dubai as "families," and people from the working class, often belonging to racialized minorities in France, who had just graduated, not found jobs, and came to Dubai to try their luck. Without elaborating on the results of this research here, it discusses various aspects of the complex, and far from obvious, articulations between whiteness and Westernness in Dubai.

This fieldwork experience convinced me that Western residents of the Peninsula are worth studying: their complex statuses, working conditions, lifestyles, and positionalities inform us about the hierarchies that shape ur-ban societies of the Gulf. These elements differ from one context to another, for instance from Riyadh to Dubai. This heterogeneity may result from different relations to colonization and imperialism, national projects, job markets, forms and sizes of white/Western communities, status of nonnational residents, and interactions with residents having no Western passports. Fieldwork, as an embodied experience, helps us understand the construction of such status, its gendered, classed, and racialized dimensions, and blurred boundaries.

Structural Misunderstandings

To conclude this chapter, the three of us reflect on some encounters we have had as we disseminated our research to academic audiences. While many of our academic interlocutors have offered generous and constructive criticism, we have also experienced what might be called structural misunderstandings of our work. By structural misunderstandings, we refer to the ways in which misreadings of our work reflected some of the assumptions that we have been discussing in this chapter. We unpack here an experience that two of us, Ahmed and Neha, shared on a panel about the Gulf at an area studies conference, and the experience of our third author, Amélie, with academic referees as she shifted her work from Riyadh to Dubai. The overlaps in these experiences, we argue, highlight some of the ongoing erasures and exceptionalizations through which this part of the world is regionalized.

The panel on which Neha and Ahmed presented was held in one of the larger meeting halls and was well attended, attracting around one hundred people. While we presented papers on significantly different topics—Ahmed on the political and cultural geographies of Dubai leisure spaces, Neha on American higher education in the Gulf—both papers engaged with whiteness, segregation, and the legacies of Western imperialism in the Gulf region, topics that we explore in this volume and in our other published work as well. Both papers attempted to map the everyday sociocultural and geographic effects of British, and more recently American, imperial interventions in the region. One of the main points that united our papers was that racialized and Orientalist logics produce "expatriate" privilege and inform the foreign resident's role in circumscribing urban geographies of belonging and exclusion. The exploitation of migrant labor (not to mention the extraction of oil) produces profit for multinational corporations and provides high-paying jobs for a large number of (white) Western foreign residents. This is not at all disconnected from modes of labor within British colonialism and American oil imperialism (see the more detailed discussion in the introduction and chapter 4).

Our two papers taken together were not well received by a small but vocal number of self-identified white American audience members who had themselves worked in the Gulf for a number of years. One person seemed particularly offended by what she took to be our suggestion that she was the unconscious beneficiary of race and class privilege. She argued that as a foreign national, she too was subordinate to "locals" under the kafala sponsorship system, and she was therefore not part of the perpetuation of this system, even though she made more money within it than her non-Western counterparts. She cited forms of job insecurity built into the kafala system as well as a lack of "rights" in the Gulf as evidence that seemingly absolved Westerners from the forms of racial and class privilege that we had discussed in our papers. A discussion ensued among panelists and audience members, some agreeing with these sentiments, and others pointing out ways that they had witnessed or experienced Western expatriate racism in the Gulf. The first interlocutor's response was one that we have heard often over the course of our careers. We have all written about the ways that Western and white racism and forms of privilege manifest in Dubai, for example, and even among our academic colleagues we often heard stereotyped language about certain national groups or defensive comments about why they were paid more than non-Westerners with similar qualifications. This discourse demonstrates how Western expatriates participated in stabilizing reductive categories of identity in the contemporary Gulf. While most residents and commentators presumed that there was a hierarchy in the Gulf that was derived from a combination of income, job/residence security, and access to welfare benefits, in which nationals had more privilege than expats, who in turn had more privilege than migrant laborers, this understanding collapsed ethnicity and race into wealth, and held nationals solely responsible for the system that oppresses the rest. This kind of analysis takes a notion of class derived from Western genealogies (itself reductive even in its "home" contexts) and transposes it globally. In the process, it also reproduces essentializing and static categories of residency in which Gulf Arabs are a homogeneous elite vis-à-vis a middle class racialized as Euro-American white and a working class racialized as South or Southeast Asian. The logic of such an analysis may be part of a coping mechanism by which privileged white Westerners avoid the discomfort of looking too deeply at the advantages that racialization, class, and contemporary imperial histories afford them. However, they are complicit in their silence in naturalizing contemporary power relations both between the West and the Gulf and within Gulf societies themselves. In this respect, they actively participate in the perpetuation of those imperial and racial histories. Moreover, it is simply inaccurate that Westerners are uniformly less privileged than their Khaleeji counterparts—Gulf nationals are not all wealthy and face uneven infractions on their rights vis-à-vis the state and other institutions based on factors such as gender, age, race, ethnicity, political activism, profession, and whether they have a nationality card, which allows them access to generous social welfare benefits.

As for Amélie, she would experience how deciding to focus on Westerners in the Gulf, and especially white Westerners, has made her research more controversial than when she was interpreted as a white Arabic-speaking expert on "Saudi women." Her new research is often seen as offensive or having a "denouncing tone," while she has the feeling that she is analyzing her fieldwork material and writing with the same methods as before. Anonymous reviews of her first submitted articles on Western residents in Dubai echoed the remarks heard at the conference described above. While the reviews formulated many interesting and constructive remarks, Amélie was struck by the tone of a few demands. These demands mainly questioned her analysis of the discourses of white Western residents living as families in Dubai on the live-in nannies they employed: weren't the discourses more diverse than what was acknowledged in the article?[9] What about affective relations between the nannies and their employers? What happened if the nannies that took care of the children became members of the Western families that hired them? Some of these remarks revealed a weak knowledge of the literature on domestic employees: as many studies in social science have shown, pretending that a domestic employee is a "family member" denies the relation of employment and makes it invisible, thus even more open to various abuses (on Dubai, see Mahdavi 2016). The criticism seemed based on the reviewers' personal experiences as white persons having lived abroad, rather than on expertise on the specific matter: some reviews admitted it. One reviewer, for instance, mentioned that researchers, when they conduct fieldwork abroad, may have no choice but to hire live-in domestic employees. This assumption was used to criticize the author's analysis of the white Western rhetoric of "we would prefer not to . . . but we have no choice." Some reviewers also criticized the use of whiteness as a concept and advised the author to give it up, since it was supposedly not an "emic" term. Such remarks have become challenges when submitting and rewriting articles. This perception of the discourse on white/Western residents as offensive—echoing the analysis of "white fragility" (DiAngelo 2011)—would, however, probably be even worse if the author was not white herself. We tackle the question of how researchers' perceived belongings, or assigned identities, influence peers' judgments on scholarly work and, in turn, careers in the concluding chapter.

Each of these encounters, we argue, reflected a number of hegemonic scripts that we have heard circulate among privileged expats in the field (with or without Western passports): that Gulf Arabs are passive and uniformly privileged recipients of welfare state benefits, that the country would fall apart without the hard work of people like them, and that while Westerners employing domestic laborers was something over which they had no choice and that could lead to improved intercultural relations, national citizens doing the same reflected their class privilege and even moral deficiency. This framework allows privileged immigrants to the Gulf to define their capital accumulation in relation to other nationalities through individual work ethic, while downplaying their participation in structural inequalities, often tied to skin color and national origin.

The discourses we just highlighted are typical of the production of Gulf urban and cultural spaces, and, relatedly, of the Gulf as field site. Ignoring the complexity of identity categories in this way recenters the white expat/expert in order to critique labor exploitation by Gulf Arabs, and erases non-white and non-Western foreign elites, who also benefit from Gulf immigration and employment structures. These discourses, in turn, help produce the image of liberal democratic societies as unmarked by harsh labor exploitation, ethnoracial hierarchies, and deep, often violent forms of exclusion (see Vora and Koch 2015 and the following chapters in this book). This image of the West was challenged by Neha's interviews with several Pakistani and Arab faculty members in Doha, for example, who described their immigration decisions through feelings of exclusion and fear stemming from racism and Islamophobia in the United States, despite having citizenship (Vora 2018). For each of us, especially after 9/11, this seems perfectly legitimate. Indeed, the two of us based in the United States (Ahmed and Neha) often also experience the United States and the American academy as places of exclusion, while we find comforts in the Gulf that cannot be reduced to class. Amélie's interviews with French residents in Dubai in 2015, after the shootings at Charlie Hebdo and Hyper Casher in Paris, echo Neha's interviews: many of them, who in France were identified as Muslim (whatever their actual beliefs and practices), feared the growing French Islamophobia and felt more comfortable living in Dubai (see chapter 2).

What emerged from our experiences of Riyadh, Doha, and Dubai as field sites was a cultural and imagined geography of the Gulf city that starkly contrasted that of Western-based expert knowledge of the region and ethnographic dichotomies of native/outsider, native/foreign, and field/home, even as the process of fieldwork pushed us to discover and narrate these Gulf cities through those very frames. We are interested in advancing more critical ethnographic entry points and methodologies in Arabian Peninsula studies through taking seriously how our field experiences, like all field experiences, are always marked by excesses—excesses that, instead of being excised in the process of producing neat categories and maps, should be taken seriously as epistemological openings. De-exceptionalizing the field for us, then, means approaching space, place, and identity as problematic in the best sense of the term: as always slipping away from attempts to fix them, and as simultaneously spatial and temporal in their emergence. We also encourage, through the ethnographic and postcolonial mode of "speaking back" to the Western academic metropole, a more critical analysis of the ways that belonging and residency in so-called "liberal" spaces need to center rather than marginalize the experiences and knowledge produced by "halfie" anthropologists and interstitial interlocutors, those who are neither at home nor away here or there, and who are both too authentic *and* not objective enough to establish as much expert or native authority as their peers. This recentering encourages new ways of seeing urban space as well, denaturalizing belonging and the built environment in order to better understand the variety of ways that people make the city, or make multiple cities that may go unnoticed by normative ethnographic cartographies and categories.

Notes

Portions of this chapter were previously published as a conversation between Ahmed and Neha on conducting fieldwork in Dubai. N. Vora and A. Kanna, "De-exceptionalizing the Field: Anthropological Reflections on Migration, Labor, and Identity in Dubai," *Arab Studies Journal* 26, no. 2 (2018): 74–100.

1. See Vora and Koch 2015 for a critique of both ethnocracy and kafala as analytic categories to understand the Arabian Peninsula.

2. See Coles and Walsh 2010; Kanna 2014; Vora 2015; and Walsh 2010 on the complex meanings of expatriate belonging in postcolonial Gulf cities. Our work resonates with this slice of Gulf migration literature while also drawing on valuable contributions in migration studies such as Fechter and Walsh 2010 and Knowles 2007 on expatriate identities and the production of whiteness in British imperial and postcolonial contexts.

3. As I discuss in chapter 4, my conversations with foreign working-class immigrants also revealed complex but highly mundane everyday lives, with little interest in the glossy supermodern images of the city.

4. Because every sojourn was between one and four months and I had limited funding, this was the best option. However, transportation in the DQ was very complicated for me, as it was surrounded by checkpoints, and taxis not carrying passengers could not enter it in order to pick up customers who lived there.

5. Sahwa means the Islamic awakening and designates a broad movement that began in the 1960s and was highly popular in the 1980s.

6. Unlike my coauthors, I did not stay in the Arabian Peninsula for very long periods. This was mainly because of visa issues in Riyadh (I stayed there about twelve months altogether, but the longest sojourn was four months long), and because of financial and personal limits in Dubai.

7. Analysis by other social scientists tends to support my feeling of constraining norms of conduct among white residents in Dubai. The geographer Katie Walsh (2007) has written that she emphasized, consciously and unconsciously, her white, feminine, and heterosexual identity while doing fieldwork among British residents in the city.

8. It was valid for one month when I did my fieldwork, and is now valid for three months.

9. Such discourses are evoked in chapter 2.

Chapter 2

How Western Residents in Riyadh and Dubai Produce and Challenge Exceptionalism

Amélie Le Renard

Many so-called Western residents in the Arabian Peninsula see themselves as outsiders vis-à-vis the societies they live in. They look at them and comment on them as if they were looking at a show. In other words, they see themselves as passive spectators of social dynamics and hierarchies. By Western residents, I mean those designated (and often self-designated) as such in Gulf cities, a status that has blurred boundaries and differs from one context to another. Inspired by one of the main ideas of Said's *Orientalism* (1978), according to which the essentialist vision of the Orient has shaped the meaning of the West, this chapter shows how exceptionalist discourses contribute to the production of distinctive Western subjectivities, and thus social groupings and hierarchies, in two cities of the Arabian Peninsula: Riyadh and Dubai.

Exceptionalist discourses represent urban societies of the Peninsula as radically different from any other society. When describing the societies of the Arabian Peninsula in these ways, the speakers implicitly position themselves as neutral judges; sometimes, however, they explicitly define themselves as

"Westerners." This status reveals complex coformations of class, race, and nation (Bacchetta 2015). In this fieldwork-based chapter, I analyze the complex positionalities of Western inhabitants of these two cities through their exceptionalist and, more rarely, antiexceptionalist discourses. As my interviews reveal, some exceptionalist discourses echo Orientalist tropes, especially through their repeated references to gender (sexism and women's oppression) and to temporality (backwardness). These discourses rely on the idea that the Gulf is disconnected from the West in terms of space and temporality. They reveal a racializing world vision marked by the "denial of coevalness" (Fabian 1983).

As the previous chapters have shown, the media and the academy play a huge role in the production of exceptionalist discourses about the Arabian Peninsula. My intention is not to exceptionalize in turn the Western residents' discourses on the societies they live in: their discourses are not isolated. While conducting research on young Saudi women's lifestyles in Riyadh, I was struck by the remarks I heard among some French residents on expatriate contracts I met there, about Saudi backwardness and women's oppression. However, they were not that different from remarks I heard in academic milieus. When I decided to pay attention to Western residents' discourses, it was also a way for me to question my approach as a white person with French nationality, living and working in France, trained in Arabic, and going to the Arabian Peninsula to do research in societies I had not lived in previously. Those inhabitants of the Arabian Peninsula who grew up in European and North American countries and settle there for a few years have until the past decade received little attention in academia, especially given the context of the abundant literature on migration and ethnicity (Kanna 2014; Vitalis 2007; Vora 2012, 2014b, 2018; Walsh 2006, 2007, 2012). Longva, in her important book on Kuwaiti ethnocracy, writes about the way in which "Western identity was a third option for middle-class migrants who could not claim the privileged Kuwaiti status but who, at the same time, refused to be caught in the ordinary category of migrant workers" (1997, 136–137). While it is useful to de-essentialize Western identity, the risk might be to elude the structural advantages, especially in terms of salary, of people with actual Western passports living and working in Gulf countries. Academics, especially those participating in Middle East/Gulf studies, have rarely questioned the advantages that a Western passport, particularly when combined with whiteness, confers.

This chapter aims to analyze exceptionalist discourses in two different social contexts and configurations of power, based on two research projects.
The first one, for which I conducted fieldwork mainly in 2012, focused on
nationalization policies in a multinational, joint-venture Saudi-French bank
in Riyadh; I call it bank A. After about forty interviews in the bank with
male employees of various nationalities and female Saudi employees (the bank
did not hire non-Saudi women), Euro–North American managers' discourses on Saudi (male and female) employees caught my attention and I
decided to analyze them in detail (Le Renard 2014b).

The second research project, for which I conducted fieldwork between
2012 and 2015, initially focused on Western residents in Dubai's professional
organizations; however, lifestyles, domesticities, and sociability became a
prominent part of the research over the course of the ninety-eight interviews
I conducted. In the second phase of this research I decided to focus on people
with French nationality, in order to deepen my analysis of the articulation
between race and nation and of the circulations of racial categories between
France and the UAE.[1] While this chapter mainly quotes French interviewees, all interviews have informed it.

Here, I analyze two prominent themes within the narratives I collected
among residents with French passports: backward sexism in Saudi Arabia,
on the one hand, and slavery-like exploitation in the Emirates, on the other
hand. I show how these themes are central in forging distinctive Western subjectivities in these two contexts. These two tropes construct the widespread
self-representation of Westerners as outsiders who are more advanced, both
professionally and morally. This self-representation is central in the formation of distinct groups and identities.

Expatriation, White/Western Subjectivities, and Exceptionalism

Two fields of literature have inspired this chapter: studies of Orientalism and
neo-Orientalism, and postcolonial approaches of expatriation and white migrations. Through the concept of Orientalism, Edward Said (1978) argued
that European representations of so-called Oriental peoples and cultures as
homogeneous, radically different, inferior, and backward had been central
to the self-affirmation of Western identity and superiority. Feminist authors (Lewis 2004; Yegenoglu 1998) have shown how the image of women

as oppressed, passive, silent, and sexualized was a fundamental trope of Orientalist discourse. They have also nuanced Said's relatively monolithic vision of Orientalism by exploring how gender and class have mediated European representations (Abu-Lughod 2001; Lewis 1998; Melman 1992; Weber 2001). Many authors have discussed the continuities between past and present discourses on the "Orient" and "Islam." Activists and politicians who are currently engaged in "moral crusades" to save Muslim women reproduce, to some extent, colonial and orientalist tropes of passive oppressed women (Abu-Lughod 2013). The concept of neo-Orientalism has been used to describe this current discursive formation that focuses on Islam and contributes to the construction of Islamophobia (Samiei 2010). As argued in the introduction, however, stereotypical representations of the Gulf include Orientalist and neo-Orientalist tropes, but go beyond them, and are not necessarily focused on Islam. The Gulf can be represented at times as the center of Muslim bigotry and fundamentalism, but also as an empty territory, or as hypermodern. Though diverse, all these representations depict the region as exceptional.

Gulf exceptionalism has various protagonists—and some detractors. While the book has focused, until now, on journalists and academics, including ourselves and our own transformations when living and conducting research in cities of the Arabian Peninsula, this chapter explores the ways in which Western inhabitants of the Gulf use exceptionalist tropes. These residents have a limited role in the production of public discourse on the Gulf. However, many are managers or employers on job markets in the Arabian Peninsula. As such, they influence the organization of labor and its hierarchies. Since academics producing social science on the Arabian Peninsula are often privileged residents in these countries, especially if they are Western passport holders, this chapter carries on, from another angle, with the reflexive approach developed in chapter 1.

Academics specializing in the contemporary Gulf have conducted research on nationals and on various communities of foreign residents, but scarcely on Western passport holders and/or on white residents. Gulf studies have been rather disconnected from works on expatriation and "white migrations" (Lundström 2014). One aim of this chapter is to contribute to bridging this gap in the wake of other authors (Coles and Walsh 2010; Vitalis 2007; Vora 2012, 2014b; Walsh 2006, 2007, 2012). Postcolonial approaches to expatriates are especially inspiring in this regard (Fechter and Walsh 2010; P. Leonard 2010; Lundström 2014). Such approaches shed light on the privileges experienced by expatriates. They also explore the various ways that whiteness is co-constructed with other forms of belonging, and transformed in migration. In this chapter, I consider Western residents as inhabitants of the Gulf interacting with the societies they live in, and developing forms of belonging, like other foreign residents (Vora 2013a). I chose to include among interviewees nonwhite Western passport holders, in order to study both the specific privileges of white residents and the blurred boundaries of Westernness in the Gulf.

Based on literatures on Orientalism and on expatriation, my approach is to analyze the interviewees' discourses and representations by taking into account their trajectories and positions in terms of gender, race, class, and nation. The intention is not to homogenize Western/white residents but to explore how they appropriate specific exceptionalist tropes depending on their backgrounds and their professional and personal situations. I argue that exceptionalist discourses shape specific, distinctive, Western subjectivities. At the same time, class, race, and gender mediate and complicate Western residents' representations and subjectivities. In particular, having a working-class and/or racialized background helps some of these residents go beyond exceptionalist tropes and thus question Western distinction.

Westerner as a Privileged Status Constructed through Structural Advantages

I am not interested in reifying the West as a category but rather in seeing what processes lead to the formation of the Westerner as a form of bounded sociality, and of Western as a frequent word used to describe people in globalizing cities such as Dubai and Riyadh. Most research on the West as a category has analyzed its occurrence in intellectual histories and official ideologies (Bonnett 2004); through both research projects, I have been looking at the category of Westerner (and, to a lesser extent, Westernized) in a sociological way, asking how the term is used and what this use reveals about social hierarchies in terms of class, race, gender, and nation.

As I argue in a book in French titled *Le privilège occidental* (*The Western Privilege*) (Le Renard 2019a), "Westerner" is never an exclusive status or identity; it is a shifting category with blurred boundaries, especially in Dubai, a city where, as in many global cities, people often have more than one passport.

While this term gathers people with diverse trajectories, and whose nation-alities evoke various histories, the majority of them benefit from structural advantages compared with other foreign residents, though their status and sociological characteristics differ in Riyadh and in Dubai. The concept of structural advantages, developed and widely used in whiteness studies and in masculinity studies (Connell 1995; Frankenberg 1993), emphasizes what is offered to a person as a consequence of their privileged position in social hierarchies. Shared structural advantages help construct dominant social groups.

In Dubai, important advantages in the job market result from having a "Western passport," an expression I often heard while doing fieldwork: though "the West" is certainly not a country and thus there is no Western passport per se, the use of the expression translates an actual social differen-tiation. In Dubai, it is widely known that having or not having a Western passport engenders very different levels of salaries in most organizations; moreover, it is an informal prerequisite for certain management jobs. In Ri-yadh, nationality determines salary in some sectors, like health, but it was not so clear in bank A, according to the employees I met. Many stated that nationality was an influential factor, but in other ways, on positions and careers. However, the employees with Western passports working in bank A were on expatriate contracts, signed in their home countries, which made their working conditions different from those of most employees: their con-tracts fell under a different law. For instance, French expatriates could not be dismissed easily, as the French labor law is (until now) relatively constrain-ing in this matter: it guarantees an advance notice and various benefits de-pending on the case. In contrast, foreign employees on local contracts can be dismissed very easily and have few rights in this case. French employees on expatriate contracts had many other advantages, such as subsidized housing, schooling for their children, airplane tickets to their home country every year, and so on. Here, I focus on people who had been living most of their lives in Western countries before moving to the Arabian Peninsula as adults. The residents that grew up in the region and got a Western passport when study-ing abroad, for instance, may have adopted discourses on the Gulf that op-pose those analyzed here.

In Riyadh and Dubai, the Western residents I met did not have exactly the same status. Most Western residents in Saudi Arabia were either men with high-paying jobs, residency, and easy access to all facilities, or women married to these men and having no job outside of housework. In other words, many of them conformed with the labor division between spouses analyzed in other contexts of white migrations (Coles and Fechter 2012). While there are also single Western residents that may have less homogeneous profiles, including a minority of single North American women working as nurses and English teachers, the Western expatriates' milieu in Saudi Arabia has not been transformed in the same way as in neighboring countries. Since firms consider Saudi Arabia a difficult country and encounter challenges in finding candidates that are ready to work and live there, the men employed there often get very attractive packages as expatriates, including bonuses for their acceptance of living in Saudi Arabia. They are encouraged to settle there with their families, and most of them live in securitized compounds (i.e., gated communities), especially in the aftermath of the attacks that took place in the 2000s, some of which targeted Westerners.[2] When I conducted fieldwork in 2012, wives rarely found stable, full-time jobs in the country, since the local market was almost completely closed to foreign women, except for specific professions such as nurse, maid, and teacher.

In the Emirates, the people I met had heterogeneous characteristics and statuses. Walsh (2006) has underlined the diversity of British residents in Dubai. Some of the residents I met lived in very privileged, even luxurious, conditions, while others got modest salaries; a few had serious problems with their employers, like not getting paid the full contracted amount or being obliged to work without a residence visa (i.e., illegally). Among the fifty-eight residents with French nationality that I interviewed, fewer than half were white. The interviewees with French nationality who were married, had children, and lived as "families" in Dubai were almost all white, in most cases they or their partners were on expatriate contracts, and they often came from middle and upper classes. Those who lived in Dubai as "single," both men and women, had more diverse backgrounds in terms of class, and, in general, less advantageous professional positions. Many of them belonged to racial minorities in France.

This chapter explores how exceptionalist discourses are deployed in two different configurations of power. In Riyadh's multinational bank, French male managers' discourses take on their full meaning in their competition with Saudi male managers. In Dubai, where the French residents I met were not in competition with national residents in the professional world, those who adopted exceptionalist discourses often aimed to justify their advantageous position; others criticized such discourses. My interviews suggest that the ways in which French residents in Dubai confirm exceptionalist discourses or call them into question depend on their own social trajectories in terms of class, race, and nation.

Exceptionalist Discourses on Sexism in a Multinational Bank in Saudi Arabia

In Saudi Arabia, as in other Gulf countries, the migration policy, and more generally, the national ideology, strictly separates foreign residents from the national population. The distinction between nationals and foreign residents is partially inscribed on spaces and bodies through official dress codes and segregation rules. In bank A, the dress code differentiated, among males, Saudis, who had to wear "thoub and shemagh or ghutra" (such dress is compulsory for Saudi men in many administrations and firms), and non-Saudis, who had to wear "shirt with necktie, trousers" and "a jacket . . . when receiving or visiting customers." "Ladies" were treated as a third category, apparently unmarked in terms of nationality—but in fact, all female employees were nationals.

Beyond the national/nonnational divide, however, there is a strict hierarchy among foreign residents. The structural advantages of Westerners in the private sector of Saudi Arabia have a long history. Robert Vitalis (2007) has analyzed how Aramco, the US firm that exploited oil in the eastern province, was organized on a nationality- and race-based hierarchy. For many decades in Saudi Arabia as in neighboring countries, expertise has been associated with Westernness and whiteness. Though the hierarchy between nationals and nonnationals has been deeply transformed since the 1950s, especially with the massive migrations from Arab and Asian countries, I heard many times during my fieldwork among Saudi employees that the foreigners were "controlling the private sector." These words often targeted Westerners. By saying that, Saudi employees were contesting the historically built association between Westernness and expertise.

Nowadays, among foreign residents, Westerners, who are a slight minority, have a specific status. Residential segregation limits the contact between nationals and most foreign residents, except for domestic employees that live in their employers' homes. "Compounds" (gated communities) where Westerners live are most often forbidden to Saudis (i.e., Saudis cannot live there, though they can visit).[3] In compliance with instructions by police authorities, no Saudi national is allowed to the "hash," a leisurely institution for expatriates in Riyadh, an open meeting taking place every Friday for foreign residents to get together and have fun in the desert. All this encourages Western residents to think of themselves as a group that radically differs from Saudis. In other words, various state and private institutions such as the labor ministry, the municipality, police authorities, firms, and compounds play a role in producing distinct sociabilities and subjectivities between Saudis and foreigners.

As far as I could observe, many Westerners in Saudi Arabia are disciplined subjects of the anti-integration policy, in contrast with other groups of foreign residents that develop hybrid identities and forms of belonging (Thiollet 2010). In bank A, for instance, I met a Pakistani manager who was in his fifties at the time of the interview. He explained to me that he had gone back to Pakistan after twenty-five years living in Riyadh, then had come back to Saudi Arabia and decided to wear the *thoub*, like Saudi nationals. His whole narrative questioned the frontier between Saudis and non-Saudis: he considered that it was socially allowed for him to wear the thoub as a long-term resident in Saudi Arabia speaking Arabic fluently. He underlined that some Saudis had Pakistani origins, thus transgressing the dominant discourse equating Saudiness with essentialized Arabness.

In contrast, the Western managers I met in bank A did not develop such hybrid subjectivities and forms of belonging. After signing their contracts as high-ranking managers, they occupied dominant positions in a country about which they knew little and where they would stay for only a few years. They used exceptionalist discourses as simple keys to understand a society in which they had occupied leadership positions immediately after their arrival. While their tendency to avoid complexity and to deliberately ignore that they might not understand everything may be seen as typical of white masculinities in management positions, working in a context perceived as non-Western probably reinforced it. They adopted reasonings and states of mind typical of imperialism, which has often—historically and until now—relied on simplified readings of concerned societies, and reductive categories and interpretations (Said 1978). Through exceptionalist discourses on Saudi men and women, these managers identified with an image of distinctive Western masculinity seen as professional, neutral, nonsexist, and nonracist.

These discourses, here, are to be understood in the context of the nationalization of job policies conducted by the Saudi Ministry of Labor in order to reduce the Saudis' high unemployment rate. The principle is to replace nonnational employees with nationals, especially in qualified, high-paying sectors through various constraining measures. In the process, Western expatriates are often solicited as "experts" in charge of transferring skills to "locals," as Vora (2014b) has analyzed in Qatar. In other words, the nationalization of jobs as a policy does not break with the construction of Westerners as experts, but renews it.

The banking sector has been a target of nationalization policies for a long time. In bank A in 2012, the nationalization rate was about 80 percent. However, it was higher in branches than in the head office, where I conducted my research.[4] Western managers were not seriously threatened by this policy. They were in Saudi Arabia on expatriate contracts: had they lost their positions in Riyadh, they would have been transferred somewhere else. Even this was unlikely, since they were the decision makers in the organization. What nationalization policies changed for Western managers was mostly that they had more and more Saudi colleagues, at all levels of professional hierarchy. Some of their subordinate colleagues were Saudi women. The nationalization of jobs, as well as a more general discourse promoting women's participation in the workforce (Le Renard 2014a), has engendered the progressive employment of Saudi women in banks, and they represented about 10 percent of the workforce in bank A.

The Western managers I met in the bank talked about their Saudi colleagues in terms of a dichotomy between "us" and "them." This is how one of them, a manager in his forties living in Riyadh with his wife and their two teenage children, justified the fact that he did not frequent any of his Saudi colleagues' homes: "I am not interested in going to a colleague's place to smoke shisha among guys, you see. . . . They are scarcely with their spouses, they see each other among [men] friends, their schedules are staggered compared to ours. . . . Men and women don't invite each other, [and they don't invite people if] it is not the same tribes. . . . And I am not interested in being among guys. We were not prepared for that in the West, we like it to be convivial [he alludes here to the presence of women]."

Here, the interviewee reinforced the national/nonnational divide through his own identification with the West and his expression of the belief in two different and incompatible civilizations. Gender and sexuality were central in this imagined dichotomy between "us" (Westerners) and "them" (Saudis), as a basis for such civilizational discourse, which echoes other colonial and postcolonial discourses on gender in Middle Eastern societies (Abu-Lughod 1998, 2013). For this man, the relations between men and women among Saudis were too "complicated," a word that he repeated several times during the interview. He associated with this "complication" "tribes" and "prayer," thus recycling classical tropes of Orientalist imagination. He defended a certain heteronormative order, in which spouses must spend their time together, and in which women must be accessible to men—a heteronormative order whose association with modernity is far from new (Najmabadi 2005).

Exceptionalist and gendered stereotypes were often deployed about the bank's employees. According to several Western male managers, Saudi males were lazy, incompetent, and too sensitive and affective. Saudi females were judged more efficient, initiative-taking, responsible, and motivated. The stereotype of the lazy Saudi man is not specific to Western managers and can also be found in reports that uncritically quote interviews with Saudi and non-Saudi entrepreneurs and CEOs as reliable sources on the local workforce. These stereotypes have impacts: in the context of the nationalization of jobs, Western managers played an important role in the selection of Saudis who got jobs in the bank, and in the selection of those who could have rising careers. Several managers saw themselves as having a mission in the organization and beyond, in a country seen as backward, notably in terms of sexism and racism. A consultant working full time for the organization told me:

> There have been new hires recently . . . especially Layla and Nura, have you met them? These two women are very Westernized in their behavior and professional culture. They are refreshing! . . . They completely disregard the separation between men and women. This is thanks to French managers. Like Pierre, who has wished to hire women in these positions in order to change women's image in the organization. Two years ago, women were never invited to men's meetings. The arrival of Layla and Nura in meetings changed many things! For them, there is no problem at all. For the other women, we have the feeling that they don't dare; . . . if they come, they don't speak. They are not yet able to behave freely during meetings. . . . Pierre's aim was to break the Saudis' codes . . . . In the beginning, he came up with reluctance. . . . It is a challenge . . . To show them that the collaborators' sex does not impact their competence. . . . It is also about breaking a hierarchical relation, especially for

certain Filipino and Pakistani expatriates that do not find their places in the organization, and at the same time wallow in their dominated position. Because in general, the expatriates' position is not more enviable than the women's position. It is better to be a Saudi woman than a Pakistani man. The dominant/dominated behavior is very strong.

This discourse describes "the Saudis' codes" as sexist and racist. Here, the consultant describes French managers as neutral judges of sexism and racism in the organization, and as more advanced outsiders who came to help and had a positive impact. Such representations imply disconnected temporalities between France (or, more generally, the "West") and Saudi Arabia. It considers racism and sexism as attributes of Saudis and symbols of backwardness, a way through which Saudis are constructed as radically other and racialized. The reference to sexism strongly echoes colonial discourses, especially those of French colonizers and their insistence on the "woman question" in Algeria. Many works have shown how this question has been used as an argument to denounce the supposed backwardness of colonized societies (L. Ahmed 1992; Alloula 1981; Clancy-Smith 2006; Lalami 2008).[5] About Saudi women in bank A, two different stereotypes are deployed. The majority of women are seen as not daring enough and not "freed"; however, two of them are described as "Westernized," and, thus, their presence is described as important in order to change the organization.

During interviews, I noted that many Saudi male managers, and a few Saudi female employees, could also use exceptionalist discourses, though in different ways. Many of them described the Saudi society as backward, but they saw the joint venture bank as an exceptional, "multicultural," and "cosmopolitan" space gathering "different," liberal, and enlightened Saudis. Many saw their own society as closed and the bank as open. They defined themselves as "open-minded," and their work in a multinational bank was an important element in constructing this self-definition.

Despite these discourses, the organization was male dominated and most Saudi women were confined to low positions. All division and department heads were either Saudi or European men, except for one Pakistani man. The subdivision heads (i.e., the level below) were men with passports from Saudi Arabia, other Arab countries, or Asian countries. Only one Saudi woman had a high management position when I conducted my research. In brief, all male Western passport holders had high positions, while male employees with Saudi, Indian, Pakistani, Filipino, Jordanian, or Palestinian nationalities were at all levels.[6]

When I interviewed the women who had reached management positions, almost all of them underlined the role of a Saudi mentor who had trusted them and helped them. Only one of the French managers was mentioned as somebody who had helped a female employee making a career. Most managers deployed discourses that praised Saudi women but did little in practice to support them. Some French managers worked at levels where they mostly interacted with men. Others' narratives of daily work in the bank, during interviews, betrayed their lack of interest in the promotion of women, despite their claims on the matter. There was the case, for instance, of a manager who was in charge of developing new training teams for employees working in branches—there are two parallel networks of branches, one that is mainly for men (with only male employees) and one only for women (with only female employees). When I asked this manager if he had male and female training teams, he admitted that his team was exclusively composed of men, and targeted only male employees. He planned to create a similar team for women, but he saw this as a "second step."

Given their lack of initiatives in practice to promote women, I interpret the French managers' discourses as ways to position themselves vis-à-vis their Saudi colleagues. Their narratives about Saudi men's sexism reproduce a fantasy that is as old as colonization: white men are saving brown women from brown men (as enunciated by Gayatri Spivak). However, we are not, here, in the context of a colonized country. I see those discourses as aimed to legitimize Western white men's supremacy in a professional world where it is partly contested, through the nationalization of jobs and the debates that surround it among Saudis. Their discourses on Saudi women, similar to colonial discourses on Middle Eastern/Third World women (Abu-Lughod 1998; Mohanty 1984), are deployed in a configuration of contested imperialism. The contestation mainly comes from Saudi citizens, not from the state: Western white men are not the main target of the nationalization of jobs policy, and may even be asked for expertise to recruit or train Saudi employees. In the competition between French and Saudi top managers, women are discursively treated as objects that justify the intervention of the former. This is mainly a discourse. No measure is taken to compensate for women's lack of presence in managerial positions, and female employees have to find their own strategies to evolve in the organization.

While the pro–Saudi women discourses do not influence their actual positions in the organization, they have an impact on the specific gender norms that are promoted for Saudi female employees. The official dress code sets strict standards concerning women's dress, but the Western managers, together with a few Saudi managers, set their own informal rules for female employees in the head office. During interviews, as mentioned before, Western managers often described the few women they worked with as "Westernized" and "freed" mainly in terms of their dress. Such words revealed which femininities these managers valued. In their discourses, being Westernized and freed almost appeared as a skill. This normative expectation, however, concerned only women: being Westernized was praised for women but rarely mentioned for men.

Female employees' dress impacted their careers. Human resources employees told me that many male managers, especially Westerners but also some Saudis, refused to work with women who covered their faces, as the overwhelming majority of the Saudi women living in Riyadh did at the time of my research. In the managers' opinion, the niqab was a symbol of both oppression and backwardness, and above all, they wanted to be able to see the faces of the women they worked with. A few Saudi managers, who saw themselves as cosmopolitan, also tried to distinguish themselves from what they described as Saudi customs, and praised the women that they described as Westernized.

Exceptionalist discourses had consequences. Given these stereotypes and their circulation in the organization, Western managers influenced which women were selected, first, to work at the head office and second, to make careers. Not only were these women excellent English speakers, which is compulsory in Saudi Arabia's joint venture banks, but they also had to present themselves and behave in a specific way, seen as Westernized and freed. These criteria excluded most of them. Yet, banking was one of the only private sector fields where Saudi women could make a career. Almost all of those who had successful career paths in banks came from upper-middle-class liberal families. Western managers played an important role in selecting the "good" nationals in the framework of nationalization policy. Those selected experienced a strong normative pressure. They were expected to embody a specific model of femininity, which was constraining. One of them, for instance, explained to me that she had to lie to her white Western colleagues about her life outside the bank, to conform to the image that they projected on her. She would invent imaginary reasons for not seeing them outside of the bank, rather than explaining that such encounters were not correct in her parents' opinion. She was dealing with contradictory injunctions between so-called Westernized femininity and her parents' definition of respectability. She explained how embarrassed she was when faced with inappropriate questions from her British boss and his wife about her lifestyle as a Saudi woman, asking her what she wore under her 'abaya, for instance. It was also one reason why she limited extraprofessional contacts.

The exceptionalist, gendered discourses of Western managers about Saudis in general and Saudi so-called sexism and backwardness in particular produced a hierarchy between those women apparently conforming to "exceptional" customs and those that behaved, within the bank's space, in different ways, often labeled as Westernized or freed. For sure, other white Western expatriates in Riyadh must have more complex visions of Saudi society. This was the case for some North American female nurses I met, who, because of their daily work, could not ignore the Saudis' actual lives in their thickness and ordinariness. Being a white, male top manager in a multinational bank, with luxurious life conditions, probably reinforced an assertive tone and a feeling of superiority. However, the discourses of Western male top managers in bank A reminded me of those I heard at the French embassy or among some male researchers in Riyadh. They constituted a sort of common sense that Western residents transmitted to each other, and through which they interpreted their interactions with Saudis. Doubts were rarely, if ever, expressed.

Exceptionalist Discourses on Exploitation in Dubai

Westerners' discourses on Emirati nationals differed from those I heard in bank A, since, in the first place, most people did not work with Emiratis on a daily basis—they were almost physically absent from the private organizations where most of my interviewees worked.[7] In fact, not meeting Emiratis was a source of frustration for some interviewees. This was the case with Stephanie, a forty-five-year-old woman. She received me in the luxurious villa on Palm Island (a very expensive area) where she lived with her husband, teenage child, and domestic employee. When I told her about my research, she expressed her surprise at my choice to study Western residents in Dubai. She said that it would be much less "exotic" than "Saudi women" (an expression meant to evoke my PhD research). Later in the interview, she told me she loved living in Dubai but regretted the "closed" character of the Emirati society. She had no Emirati female friends (in general, she did not look for friendships with men) and thought it was because women were locked up. During other interviews, two women in their forties similarly anticipated that I would ask them about their relations with Emiratis. If I did not study the Emiratis directly, then the subject of my research on Western residents must have been their relations with Emiratis. I observed afterward that a specific profile of interviewees harbored such expectations: white middle-aged married women who had several experiences of "expatriation" (i.e., spending a few years in several countries under the expatriate contracts of their husbands) and belonged to the upper class (in France and in the Emirates).[8] Such expectations revealed that, for them, Emiratis were the only "real" inhabitants that research in the Emirates could possibly focus on, a discourse also present in academia (Vora 2013a). Their quest for authenticity ended in disappointment.

Two of these women also expressed the idea that their own lives were not "interesting" for my research. This statement can be interpreted in two ways. On the one hand, women, especially when they do not make professional careers, are socialized to internalize such judgments about themselves. Living in Dubai, a neoliberal city where expatriates tend to consider each other in light of their professional positions, may reinforce this socially constructed tendency to self-deprecation. But statements such as "I am uninteresting" or "I am like everyone" also define normativity: these women were wondering why I was willing to interview them since they were "normal" (i.e., not "exotic"). Here, these women's remarks revealed what they saw as the norm: being a white heterosexual couple living in Dubai, the husband working for a multinational, the wife taking care of the kids and sometimes having a part-time professional activity. Since they were "normal" expatriates and not exotic, there was nothing to study. I would have done better going to mosques, palaces, or construction sites. Such self-representation revealed a specific, contextual, and gendered construction of whiteness in Dubai. It should be noted that not all white women held such discourses, and especially not the women who had come to Dubai in order to make a career. Among women, marriage and full-time professional activity, statuses that often excluded each other, made a difference. That said, ambiguous self-deprecations by white upper-class married women contrasted with the attitudes of some of the white male high-ranking managers interviewed in Riyadh and quoted above, who felt legitimate enough to give me a course on (their vision of) Saudi society. Even during interviews, they went on performing the expert role that justified the structural advantages they benefited from. The interlocking of gender and whiteness shaped differentiated expatriate subjectivities and exceptionalist discourses, marked by normative curiosity or seemingly authoritative assertions about the "locals."

Most exceptionalist discourses I heard among Western residents in Dubai did not focus on Emiratis but rather on Dubai's social order, and more specifically on what many referred to as slavery-like exploitation.[9] Here, I would like to evoke some white residents' ambivalent discourses on domestic employees. Among the residents I met, most parents raising children in Dubai (as opposed to parents who cannot afford to live in Dubai with their children) employed a live-in "nanny" or "maid" (to quote the terms they used).[10] However, many, especially women, felt obliged to justify their adoption of a practice that they judged immoral and backward. Many of them had employed live-out "nannies" or "cleaning ladies" before moving to Dubai. In Dubai, they felt particularly uncomfortable with having the worker living in their houses, and many discussed this specific aspect of the relationship during interviews. Their self-justifications helped construct their distinctive Western positionalities.

The parents I met were using three main arguments. First, almost all of them presented their decision to hire a live-in domestic employee as a constrained one, given that alternatives in Dubai (hiring a part-time nanny or enrolling their children in a childcare center) were either more expensive or more complicated. Second, many asserted that they had no influence on Dubai's social order, which they saw as exceptional and separated from their own lives. As I conducted an interview over lunch with Philippe, a high-ranking manager on an expatriate contract who invited me to his favorite pizzeria in Madinat Jumeirah (a hotel and shopping complex with various expensive stores, meant to evoke an old souk), he confided that he and his wife would probably not have had a third child had they not lived in Dubai and benefited from a live-in nanny's work. Later in the conversation, he explained: "It is always important to put our vision of people in perspective with life in their countries. For instance, sometimes we [he refers to himself and his wife] thought that the nanny earned almost nothing, but this gave her access to a lot, at home. She was a mother, she had children in the Philippines.

It seems weird to us, but for us in France, a century ago, it was the same. The system of nannies . . . So, there [in the Philippines], it's the grandparents who bring up the children."

Philippe's discourse is a good example of a world vision marked by the "denial of coevalness" (Fabian 1983)—that is, the denial that he and the nanny live in the same time. In other words, Philippe situates the nanny's life in the past, relative to a present conceived as Western, or even French. According to Philippe's teleological vision of history, the Philippines, which he associates with the nanny's life conditions in Dubai, is less advanced than France on the way to development and social justice—one century backward. This "other" time to which the nanny supposedly belongs implies the existence of an "other" space, disconnected from Philippe's situation, as if different societies followed parallel paths that never met—a narrative that, of course, blatantly ignores the various forms of colonialism and imperialism that have shaped contemporary situations, including Philippe and his wife's daily life in Dubai. According to this imaginary of disconnected times and spaces, revealed by Philippe and other interviewees, Western residents would not participate in the exploitation they denounce, since they would not live in the same time as nannies.

The third argument used to justify the employment of a live-in nanny also relates to exceptionalism. Some interviewees represented themselves as saviors compared with "local," "Emirati," or "Arab" employers, presented as exploitative.[11] Philippe, for instance, said "an expat pays a nanny twice as a local, while he makes her work twice less." As for Stephanie, she explained: "Beside her salary, I buy her food separately, to make sure that she does not save on what she is eating. . . . Filipino women speak a lot with each other, she speaks with her friends, and the main objective is to not work for Arab families, whatever the nationality, because . . . some of her friends work in conditions that are close to slavery."

These discourses tend to present the relation of employers with nannies as a charitable one, rather than a relation of employment. Such discourse shapes a twofold distinction. On the one hand, it reinforces social distance and hierarchy between employer and employee. It portrays the latter as disempowered and needing help. On the other hand, these people also assert social distance toward "other" employers of nannies, described as "Arabs," "locals," or "Emiratis." The relations these "local" employers have with domestic employees are described as exceptionally exploitative, slavery-like.

In Dubai, the parents I interviewed felt it was necessary to assert their attachment to equality, social justice, and nonexploitation. In France, employers of nannies do not hold similar discourses about the relation they have with their employees (Ibos 2008). The discourses that employers develop in Dubai define equality as a Western value. Many of them explained, significantly, that they would not stay in Dubai when their children became teenagers, in order for the latter not to internalize "bad" values. "Bad" values most often referred to stark inequality, to slavery-like exploitation, and sometimes to the limits constraining the interactions between boys and girls, in contrast with perceived freedom in their home countries. Through Westernness and its supposed "values," they built a positive, distinctive identity while at the same time considering themselves as normal, unmarked, white "classical" expatriates. Many single residents with no children expressed similar perceptions of slavery-like employment, though they did not experience the same dilemmas as parents, as they were not allowed, as singles, to hire full-time domestic workers.

Antiexceptionalist Counternarratives

In Dubai, I heard several counternarratives criticizing exceptionalist discourses. These counternarratives were responses to both media representations considered as stereotypical and remarks that friends or relatives in the home country addressed to residents in Dubai about their choice to live and work in this city. Counternarratives came up during interviews, as my position as a sociologist from France was often assimilated to those two figures (a journalist and/or an acquaintance coming from the home country). The arguments used to deconstruct exceptionalist discourses either referred to globalization or were a criticism of the French social order, especially in terms of racism and, though less frequently, sexism.

Christophe, a thirty-five-year-old white man who had grown up in the working class in France, proposed to meet me in a shopping mall close to the flat where he lived with his wife and two-year-old daughter, outside the most prestigious areas of Dubai. Christophe had been living in the Gulf for ten years. In Qatar he had met his wife, a Filipina who then worked as a receptionist. After living a hedonistic lifestyle for years as a "single" resident, spending all his earnings on parties and trips with friends, as he explained to me, he was trying to "calm down" and save money for projects with his newly formed family. Christophe had kept very strong relations with his parents and went back to France every summer. On one such trip back home, he saw the friends he had grown up with. He explained:

> I can feel that some [friends] are jealous. . . . But then, "There are many positions, come and do it!" I have been working so hard for ten years, unbelievably long hours, to get what I have. I have not stolen that from anybody. . . . Every summer, we have the big clichés, people see a report on [television] and they explain to us what is happening here. Sure, there are many abuses here. . . . What I say to these people, that tell me "don't you mind working with people that are underpaid?" . . . I say "But wait, . . . you participate in the same thing every time you put gas in your car." . . . The problem with Dubai, it is that it reveals all that globalization manages to hide.

Christophe justified his position as an expatriate (i.e., working on an advantageous expatriate contract) in Dubai vis-à-vis his friends, relatives, and himself by insisting on the amount of work he had to accomplish to reach such a position. As the son of two parents who had worked in factories their whole lives, he took a stand on the exploitation of workers: he explained that he insisted on making all the risky operations himself, since he had much better health care than the workers he was supervising. Against the image of Dubai as exceptional and disconnected, he underlined that everyone, even in France, was participating in the global networks that shaped the city's economy.

Among French interviewees, some deconstructed the exceptionalist discourse on Dubai by criticizing the French social order. They constructed parallels, for instance, between the situation of their parents as immigrants in France and their own situation as immigrants in Dubai. Contrary to many upper-class white expatriates, they did not feel obliged to justify their (relative) success in Dubai—among interviewees, those who occupied the most advantageous positions in terms of salaries, packages, and responsibilities were white middle-aged upper-class men. Amin, a thirty-three-year-old man working in communications and marketing, was one of the interviewees whose narrative referred frequently to his parents, whom he described as "simple workers" and who had emigrated from Algeria to France decades ago. After completing a master's degree, Amin had not found a stable job in

France, which he explained was because of racial discrimination. Faced with unemployment and financial problems, he decided to travel to the United States in order to learn English. He managed to live there for one year, had various short-term jobs, and felt overall more valued than in France. He considered his installation in Dubai not as a choice between infinite possibilities but as a constrained choice given the impossibility of finding a job in France, a way out. Like other interviewees, he underlined that he would have preferred to stay in France, a country that he loved and did not reject, but where he could not develop his potential. While Amin was critical of Dubai's social order, he did not idealize the French social order; his narrative did not aim to oppose the Emirates and France. He saw both societies as shaped by profound, blatant inequalities. To some extent, Amin's professional success in Dubai appeared as compensating for the difficulties that he and his parents had experienced in France. His salary helped make his parents' lives easier. Amin said he sent much money to his parents, at least one-third of his salary. He commented: "This is funny, you don't pay taxes, but in the end you still send [money] to France so . . . in the end, I do pay taxes. This is my way to pay taxes. All that goes back to France."

During my latest stay, in February 2015, many interviewees described France as an exceptional place in terms of Islamophobia, while living in Dubai was experienced as a relief. The spectrum of French Islamophobia was actually omnipresent in some of the interviews I conducted at that time, like the one with Linda, a thirty-year-old woman who had lived in Dubai for four years:

> What I love in Dubai, beyond all these materialist, superficial things, and the comfort we have here, it is that I have never seen a place, at least in France . . . For instance when you go to JBR [a semi-pedestrian space by the edge of a beach, in a prestigious, commercial area], you can see, walking side by side, a Russian woman wearing mini shorts and a tank top, . . . and an Emirati woman, completely covered, under her burqa. And nobody will watch, nobody will criticize, everyone does what they want, everyone wears what they want. . . . If someone does not drink alcohol, . . . nobody is going to try to have them drink alcohol.

It is interesting to note that Linda chooses the opposition between mini shorts and burqa as the sign of a cosmopolitan, respectful society. The use of the word "burqa" to describe Emirati women's dress, a term not used in this way in the Emirates but widely used in the French media especially in the aftermath of the war on Afghanistan, reveals to what extent this discourse on freedom in Dubai is constructed in response to a long experience of Islamophobia in France. In the aftermath of the "Je suis Charlie" movement that followed the shootings at Charlie Hebdo and Hypercacher in Paris on January 7, 2015, such accounts were especially frequent in interviews with French residents in Dubai, especially some self-defined as Muslim, or to whom this religious identity was ascribed.[12] Their discourse contrasted French Islamophobia with Dubai's "tolerant" environment. A few interviewees, however, had experienced Islamophobia not only in France but also in Dubai's job market. A young man, for instance, had not obtained a job after the last interview, which took place with the CEO of the firm to which he applied. The latter believed that his short beard and the fact that he did not drink alcohol made him unsuitable for the job. Such stories—several interviewees evoked similar discrimination, though not in the first person—led these interviewees to analyze Islamophobia in the professional world as a global tendency, present in Dubai as well as in other cities in France and elsewhere.

Several women constructed a counternarrative to the discourse exceptionalizing women's status and condition in the Gulf. While many of these women's relatives had feared their moving to a region of the world seen as essentially sexist, they insisted that they felt more respected than in France, in both public and professional spaces. Their feelings can be related to Dubai's discriminatory policing of public spaces, which cannot be analyzed here in detail (Buckley 2015; Lori 2011), and to national/Western structural advantages on the job market: white/Western women, especially when they do not raise children, benefit from the essentialization of whiteness/Westernness as expertise.[13] Here again, the counternarratives were constructed in response to previous experiences of sexism in public spaces and/or professional worlds in France. Some female entrepreneurs said they felt taken seriously for the first time in their lives, especially when interacting with businessmen. Other female interviewees mentioned bad experiences, including low wages and harassment. My point here is not to argue whether a place is better or worse, but to underline that for some women, experiences were comparable.

The common feature of these counternarratives is that they partly question the usual assumption of Western superiority, manifest in exceptionalist discourses, and propose other visions of space and time. The Emirates and France are commented on through one lens. They are compared aspect by aspect. They are considered as parts of the same world, as two variants of a contemporary reality.

Conclusion: Exceptionalism versus Global Inequality

Exceptionalist discourses use several arguments, centered on men's supposed sexism and the oppression of women in Riyadh, and on slavery-like exploitation in Dubai. Beyond the content of these discourses, they reveal some aspects of Westerners' positionalities in the two cities. In both cases, the interviewees see themselves as outsiders, even when their positions, as managers in organizations or as employers of domestic workers, contradict this perception. This vision of oneself as outsider is linked to the racializing belief, often based on gender, that "locals" are radically other, and to the belief that the Arabian Peninsula and the countries where its inhabitants come from (the Philippines, India) are not currently living in the same time as the West and, thus, as Westerners. These exceptionalist and racializing beliefs allow Western residents to criticize the lack of justice and equality—in terms of gender and work relations—and to see themselves as more advanced, even as models, in these fields. In their discourses, equality is essentialized as Western, while Gulf societies are essentialized as unequal. Through a proclaimed moral sense of equality that is meant to be distinctive, these interviewees, who occupied advantageous positions, defended a form of hegemony that was thought of as better, fairer, and thus more legitimate than that of "locals" and/or "others." Besides skillful experts, they saw themselves as fair managers and employers, sometimes as saviors in a region seen as exceptionally unfair. This belief was particularly strong among white residents belonging to the upper classes. It helped construct a discourse about themselves as a specific group with distinctive identities among local elites, who have various national backgrounds.

In Dubai, many interviewees developed counternarratives that questioned this exceptionalist vision of the Gulf. Compared with the first group of interviewees, the people belonging to this second group did not occupy dominant positions in their home countries—they came more often from the working class and many belonged to racial minorities in France. Some underlined the global networks that linked the unequal social order in Dubai with the behaviors of consumers in France; others criticized unfairness in France through evoking their own experiences of racism, sexism, discrimination, and Islamophobia. Without necessarily idealizing Dubai, they used the same frameworks to analyze the situation in this city and the one they had lived in before. Many discussed and criticized the discourse of Westernness as fairness and equality. By doing so, they undermined one element of the construction of Westerners as a distinct and advantaged group in several cities of the Arabian Peninsula. Very few, however, addressed the essentialization of expertise as Western, which is the basis of the structural advantages they benefit from in the job market.

When "exceptionalist" expatriates identified with equality in contrast with various types of supposedly exceptional inequalities attributed to the Gulf, they were implicitly expressing their perception of themselves as Westerners. As for antiexceptionalist counternarratives, what made them possible was not only a different vision of the Gulf but also a different vision of Western societies. In exceptionalism, like in Orientalism, the self and the other are co-constructed through contrast and opposition. This is how complex perceptions of Western societies and a sharp awareness of global inequalities contributed to complexifying usual exceptionalist stereotypes on Gulf societies among some interviewees, building comparisons based on their own experiences.

Notes

While this chapter's argument is original, some extracts of interviews and a few sentences have been published in Le Renard 2014, 2019a, and 2019b.

1. Residents with French nationality in the UAE officially numbered 25,000 in 2015 and 30,000 in 2019. See "UAE's Population—By Nationality," BQ Magazine, April 12, 2015, http://www.bqdoha.com/2015/04/uae-population-by-nationality and "Présentation des Emirats arabes unis, *France diplomatie*, updated on May 14 2019, https://www.diplomatie.gouv.fr/fr/dossiers-pays/emirats-arabes-unis/presentation-des-emirats-arabes-unis/.

2. In the 2000s, several terrorist attacks targeted the oil industry or Western residents in Saudi Arabia. In response, the police made numerous arrests of men (especially young men) suspected to be sympathizers of jihadi movements or ideas. Many remained in prison for years without being sentenced.

3. There were exceptions to the rule, and I met Saudis living in compounds.

4. As I was conducting research in Riyadh for my PhD on young Saudi women's lifestyles and gender norms (Le Renard 2014a), I had met both a French manager working at bank A (through the French embassy) and a Saudi female employee (through personal contacts). The French manager had allowed me to conduct a few interviews in the organization during my PhD research. When I decided to develop a project on the bank after my PhD, I entered it through the people I had interviewed previously (the French manager had left in the meantime).

5. On this aspect, see also chapter 3 by Vora.

6. The jobs considered as unskilled, such as tea boys, security guards, cleaners, and call center workers, were outsourced.

7. A few interviewees worked in semipublic organizations where they had many Emirati colleagues. Some of them talked about these colleagues in a way comparable with the interviews I quoted on Saudi Arabia.

8. Wives are under the expatriate contracts of their husbands in ambiguous ways. Since the "family" is often provided for in these contracts, wives benefit from advantageous conditions while embodying a subaltern status as "dependents."

9. When the discourses focused on Emirati nationals, they included references to so-called Emirati sexism in ways similar to what I observed in Saudi Arabia about so-called Saudi sexism.

10. Parents have to earn a certain amount in order to bring their children to Dubai, legally. Raising children in Dubai is very expensive for foreign residents, as schools and insurance are private. This is one of the reasons why some parents decide not to bring their children to Dubai even if their salary is above the legal limit.

11. See also Kanna's discussion of discourses of exceptional Gulf labor exploitation in chapter 4.

12. The Sunday following the shootings, a huge march was organized in Paris around the slogan "Je suis Charlie" (I am Charlie). This slogan pressured people to declare themselves not only *against* violent shootings but also *with* the controversial satirical newspaper. The social pressure to position oneself was particularly strong for Muslims and people assigned to such religious identity.

13. Among my interviewees, the women who were married and/or raised children in Dubai faced discrimination in the job market.

Chapter 3

ANTHROPOLOGY AND THE
EDUCATIONAL ENCOUNTER

Archival Logics and Gendered "Backlash"
in Qatar's Education City

NEHA VORA

Outside the Sidra Medical and Research Center, a massive building devoted to prenatal and women's health, fourteen giant statues commissioned
by Sheikha Mayassa bint Hamad al-Thani, chairwoman of Qatar Museums
and sister of the emir, depict stages of fetal development from conception to
birth. Designed by the controversial British artist Damien Hirst, the statues,
along with their rumored $20 million price tag, caught international media
attention for their boldness in showing the naked human form in a conservative Islamic country, as well as for what was billed as yet another over-the-
top expenditure that did not make aesthetic or practical sense for Doha's
urban development. A reporter for the *New York Times*, describing the installation, wrote: "Even for a Persian Gulf country that is aggressively buy-
ing its way into modernity, this installation takes official acceptance of
Western art to a new level. Local women still adhere to centuries-old Islamic
traditions, wearing the abaya, a long cloak, and niqab, or face covering; images of women are routinely censored in books and magazines. Even the
representation of the human form is unusual" (C. Vogel 2013).

Figure 1. Photograph of *The Miraculous Journey* by Damien Hirst in front of Sidra hospital construction site, April 2014. Alexey Sergeev, asergeev.com. Reprinted with permission.

Shortly after their unveiling in 2013, the Hirst statues, collectively titled *The Miraculous Journey*, were re-covered by large cloths similar to the white spheres they had been under before they were ceremoniously displayed to the public. This is when rumors began among my colleagues within the American branch campuses of Education City about the reasons why the statues were "shrouded": "There must be some major backlash against Mayassa; she's gone too far this time," said some. "These babies remind me of those aborted fetus images I used to see on campus back home that the pro-life groups would bring," said others. "It is *haram* to display the human body in Islam," I also heard. Others felt the covered babies were creepy because they seemed dead; it would be better to just show them. The Qatar Foundation's official reason for covering them: to protect them from construction dust as the Sidra hospital was still under construction.[1] While other public art in Doha has stirred controversy among Qataris, these statues seem to have gone relatively unquestioned (Kelly 2016). Qatar Museums still highlights the statues on its web page, and there have been no attempts, as far as I know, to remove them or move them to a less prominent position on the campus.

The reactions by Western academics, who compose the majority of the professoriate within Education City's American branch campuses, highlighted their own entry into seeing fetuses: through pro-life versus pro-choice debates on college campuses for the most part, a visual reality that was not part of campus culture in a country where abortion is illegal and absent from public discourse. In addition, childhood is not publicly sexualized, so the nude form of an unborn, developing baby was relatively disconnected from adult bodily display. Circulating ideas about what was *haram*, particularly around gender and women's bodies, also highlighted the gatekeeping and culture-making practices of Western experts and consultants, and were not necessarily connected to scholarly Islamic debates or Qatari everyday practices. In addition, my colleagues' watercooler conversations and the international media coverage of this art installation, which tended to converge, included exceptionalizing judgments about choices made by Qatari leaders, judgments that implied a proper development trajectory for the country—including a proper way to balance tradition and modernity within that trajectory—and implied that Qatar (an elusive yet unified state actor) was failing at both. What would make more sense, after all, for a women's hospital in a country focused on increasing the birth rate among citizens and reducing miscarriages and birth defects than statues depicting a healthy (and male) developing fetus?

This chapter (and its title) takes its inspiration from Talal Asad's (1973) *Anthropology and the Colonial Encounter*, in which he argues that British anthropology's post–World War II turn away from holistic functionalism to more specialization, which coincided with so-called primitive societies becoming postcolonial nation-states, was not a calculated and reflexive move away from the imperial logics that shaped European academic knowledge practices but rather a naturalization and universalization of those fundamental understandings of difference. To claim that the discipline changed because the world changed did not question the inherent assumptions on which ideas about non-European people were founded; rather, it allowed those ideas to proliferate as the discipline grew and gained more academic legitimacy. Asad's call for a decolonization of anthropology was therefore not just about anthropology but about Western epistemology in much broader academic and nonacademic forms, which influenced and in turn were constituted through ethnographic encounter. Building on Asad's important intervention, I argue that the American academy and its disciplines have normalized traditional anthropological modes of understanding culture as bounded and tethered to place in order to address diversity and difference.

The anthropologization of difference in higher education—especially as universities globalize into locations that are considered the West's others—is also central to the branch campus as a space of encounter, where both Qatar and America are (re)constituted along with ideas of liberalism, illiberalism, gender, nation, ethnicity, class, sexuality, and religion. In my research, I found that the faculty and administrators within Education City, even though they tended to be more positively oriented toward the project than their US-based counterparts, often reduced Qatariness to fixed notions of culture and religion—ironically becoming themselves producers of difference through their gatekeeping practices (Vora 2018). This was evident in the explanatory frameworks that many of them deployed to understand the Hirst statues and their "shrouding"—the word most often used to describe their re-covering, which both implied death and evoked an exotic other, as well as the Orientalist gaze on the veiled female form. Culture and religion, I found, were not easily thought or taught as flexible in branch campuses, just as they were not at "home," despite the language of diversity and multiculturalism that pervaded both spaces. And they were ongoing threats to liberal success.

What counts as failure and threat, and to whom? I explore these questions in this chapter. I do so by focusing on how Qatar Foundation responded to criticisms, primarily from segments of the citizenry that felt left out of knowledge economy development, through the development of Hamad bin Khalifa University (HBKU), an umbrella national institution that over the time of my research began to encompass the branch campuses, research centers, and new universities opening in Education City, including the Sidra Medical Center. HBKU's formation reconfigured space within the Education City compound and changed my everyday mobility within it, as it did my students' and colleagues'. I explore these changes and my interlocutors' responses to them in order to consider how anthropological categories of difference and the university's approach to incorporating oppositional politics migrated along with American institutions, disciplinary formations, and faculty and administrators. While many of these changes, such as moves to segregate formerly coeducational spaces, may have appeared to Western academics as a backlash that fit into their exceptionalizing ideas of Qatari culture and gender norms, or failure of liberalism in illiberal space, oppositional logics were not always pegged to conservative religiosity but rather part of critiques of broader imperial practices within certain, and not all, parts of the country.

Nationalizing Education City: The Creation of Hamad bin Khalifa University

Education City, considered the lynchpin of Qatar's investment in "knowledge economy" development, houses branch campuses of six elite US universities: Texas A&M, Carnegie Mellon, Georgetown University Walsh School of Foreign Service, Weill Cornell Medical School, Virginia Commonwealth, and Northwestern. My research within Education City spanned between 2010 and 2014. During this time, I conducted over ten months of fieldwork, taught courses at two different institutions (Texas A&M University at Qatar for three summer sessions of Introduction to Cultural Anthropology, and the Qatar Faculty of Islamic Studies for a semester of Anthropology of the Middle East), gave several guest lectures at a range of institutions, conducted interviews and participant observation, attended conferences and talks, was invited to give public talks, and attended student events and faculty and student orientation activities. It was through my research and teaching experiences in Doha that I began to formulate the central arguments for the book that resulted from this research, about the presumptions built into notions of liberal education, as well as about the ways that anthropological understandings of culture—as bounded and essential—have been mainstreamed into the academy to prop up narratives of globalization as part of liberal crisis.

In my book *Teach for Arabia*, I explore how crisis narratives animate the majority of academic commentaries about Education City and similar American university partnerships in so-called illiberal states. These universities and the people who work in them have been met by immense skepticism by US-based academics who see the Gulf through exceptionalizing frameworks as a repressive authoritarian space riddled with human rights violations (particularly around sexuality and gender), severe economic inequality, and labor abuses, and who question how liberal education and its values of academic freedom, egalitarianism, and democracy could possibly function in such illiberal climates (see, for example, Aksan 2010; Benhabib 2011; Ross 2011). While indeed the lived realities of many people in the Gulf are marked by inequality and harsh living conditions, my work on Dubai and Doha has challenged the exceptionalism on which much knowledge production about the region relies, arguing instead that colonial and imperial encounters and contemporary global processes of migration, labor, and capital have produced relatively similar forms of inequity, uneven belongings, and exploitation in so-called liberal and illiberal spaces, as well as an investment in the idea of a world ontologically divided into these forms of culture, territory, and power (Vora and Koch 2015; see also Koch 2016 and chapters 2 and 4 of this volume). Contrary to presumptions that Gulf universities would limit critical thinking and academic freedom, I have found over the years of this project that students in the Gulf are particularly adept at challenging the unequal foundations on which Western liberalism itself rests.

Liberal higher education, like these campuses and others that have been promulgating across the region, is not only considered by Gulf leaders as central to diversifying away from petroleum reliance but also as a form of social engineering that can produce the entrepreneurial citizens required to move away from rentier state welfare structures, a bloated public sector, and the demographic "imbalance" between citizens and foreign residents. In some Gulf states, like Qatar and the UAE, noncitizens make up over 85 percent of the population and almost the entirety of the workforce, especially in the private sector. Qatari women especially are considered essential to the production of modernity and to the development of a citizen-centered workforce; however, their overrepresentation in higher education vis-à-vis national men and state-sponsored feminist development projects has also raised questions about the breakdown of "traditional" patriarchal and heteronormative gender roles, particularly through the policing of women's morality as they attempt to navigate coeducational spaces that are infused with Western values, such as those of Education City's branch campuses (Ridge 2014). Thus, there is a parallel discourse of crisis around American higher education among the Qatari citizenry.

During the years that I conducted research for this project, public debates about the pace and scale of development, the contours of Qatar's national branding, and whom modernization actually serves simmered to the surface among Doha's residents. These debates took place in Arabic and English newspapers, on television and radio shows, on university campuses, and within social media forums. Education City may not have always been the direct topic of conversation, but the Qatar Foundation understood that conversations about the country's future connected to this space as an ideological, economic, and material project. As such, the foundation spent considerable effort and money shifting both its rhetoric and its built environment since the inception of the project to better address local stakeholders.

The first branch campus, Virginia Commonwealth University Qatar, opened its doors in 1998, with the other universities following soon after. Sheikha Moza—the mother of the current emir and chairperson of Qatar Foundation—envisioned Education City (along with her husband, the former emir) at the time of its founding as a "multiversity," where the best international brands would offer their top programs in one place in order to serve Qatar's growing private sector needs. Originally a "collection of individual buildings . . . differentiated by a variety of architectural expressions" (Mitchell 2015, 44), Education City's built environment was marked by a lack of cohesiveness and inattention to use-value for students and staff. Its touted sustainability efforts, similarly, were more about international branding than actual environmental impacts, similar to other green projects in the Gulf (Günel 2019; Koch 2014; Mitchell 2015).[2] The campus was also an elite enclave gated off from the rest of Doha, governed as a free zone where some of the laws in force in the rest of the city were relaxed (Kane 2011, 123). Several of my early student and alumni interviews reflected a sense of not knowing many people outside one's university building, for the branch campuses felt rather atomized. Local controversy also began to build about Education City being inaccessible, both physically and academically, to the citizens it claimed to serve. This pushback, which intensified around the time of the Arab revolutions in 2011, led to state responses in other areas, such as doubling (or more) public sector salaries, instituting mandatory military service for men, removing alcohol from the Pearl freehold complex, slashing Qatar Foundation's budget, and increasing funding to the national public Qatar University (Ulrichsen 2014). In response to these criticisms, Qatar Foundation's planning and programming changed considerably, as did to a lesser degree that of the branch campuses. Parts of the campus were closed to car traffic to create more pedestrian- and bus-friendly corridors for students, and more greenways were built. Attempts to engage the wider community could be seen in the removal of security checks and ID requirements at gates to the compound, which took place in late 2014. Meanwhile, branch campuses and some newly opened local institutions started offering more community-based programming and courses that were regionally focused.

Perhaps the most representative of these changes was the rebranding of Education City as Hamad bin Khalifa University (or HBKU), a national university that was meant to encompass the educational and research institutions in Education City, including the American branch campuses. I first learned about HBKU when I was beginning my research in 2010. At that time, there were rumblings about a potential "local university restructuring" among my colleagues, but there seemed to be little concern about the impact it would have on the functioning of day-to-day academic life. By the time I was finishing this project in the fall of 2014, HBKU had become more centralized, and its bureaucratic presence was palpable. The new initiatives and institutions launched by Qatar Foundation under the HBKU name were met by resistance and insecurity from branch campus administrators, who felt that their institutional independence was under threat, particularly since many were undergoing contract renegotiation with Qatar Foundation under tighter budgets.[3] The formation of HBKU and the positioning of the branch campuses under its umbrella represented a solid move toward nationalization and away from the "best international brands" approach that Qatar Foundation had started with twenty years earlier. The website for Education City also reflected this turn to the local and to Qatari heritage and culture, most recently in 2016 with rebranding, a new strategic plan, and a new logo and tagline for HBKU that focused on heritage and directly mirrored the language of the Qatar National Vision 2030.[4] Vision 2030 is a forty-page document that was published in 2008 and explicitly outlines the country's focus on an indigenous postindustrial, sustainable modernity that centers citizens and certain desirable (read upper middle class and professional) expatriates, in the form of "knowledge economy" in particular.[5] It has since driven development throughout the country, especially in the education sector.

The first building to carry the HBKU name was the Student Affairs building, which completed construction in 2011. By 2014, HBKU Student Affairs had hired several administrators, including a few Qataris, and was up and running with its own programming as a vibrant space that brought students together, thus making branch campus Student Affairs officers wonder about redundancy and how to work with and across this new format. Local institutions, such as the Qatar Faculty of Islamic Studies (QFIS) and the Translation and Interpreting Institute, were pulled under the HBKU umbrella. The newly opened QFIS building, in one of the prime locations in Education City, showcases the shift away from the secular liberal enclave environment that Qatar Foundation originally intended. The building draws from Arabic architecture and is covered with Islamic script. It also includes a large mosque that is open to the public for Friday services. The institution itself, a national nonsecular graduate school whose faculty hail mostly from other Arab countries, also highlights efforts by Qatar Foundation to move away from relying solely on Western foreign institutions and liberal education. In planning for QFIS, Qatar Foundation aimed to replicate a traditional madrasa, where learning and worship take place in one space (Ahmadi 2015).

HBKU is modeled on a research university and had begun offering its own master's and postgraduate degrees, some in collaboration with branch campus faculty, when I last conducted fieldwork in 2014; more were in the planning stages. The university had also hired research faculty directly, not through any of the branch campuses or other institutions, and funded them through lucrative Qatar National Research Fund (QNRF) grants, even though these faculty had no research or teaching programs yet in operation.[6] As one person told me, the new initiatives were all aimed to create a system "skewed to force people to study more about Qatar." The focus on Qatar and Qataris was also reflected in changes in scholarship and grant mechanisms, some of which were available only to citizens or to local scholars.

For many Western expatriates working in the branch campuses, however, daily life in Education City did not feel as open or as accessible as before. When I arrived in Doha after a two-year hiatus to complete my research, I had to contend with these new changes, which on the surface might indicate the very failure of liberal social engineering in so-called illiberal space that the cautionary critiques of American university partnerships in the Gulf foretell. That semester, I was a visiting assistant professor at QFIS, where I was the only non-Muslim woman employee and the only woman faculty member. At the time, the institution's new building was still under construction so they were sharing space with other entities in another building. Though I had previously spent time in that building, I had never experienced such drastic differences between gender norms and gendered (as well as ethnoracial) policing and self-policing within the confines of the Education City campus before. For example, classrooms and other spaces in the QFIS wing had been turned into men's prayer rooms, and the call to prayer, which is not broadcast elsewhere on campus, would unevenly play out of people's phones and radios. Male colleagues policed each other, making sure they would all pray; there were unexpected faculty firings throughout the semester; and I was told after starting my position that a hijab was required— something not included in my contract and not part of Qatar Foundation's dress code. Even though QF dress code allows for short sleeves and skirts that fall at the knee, being *hijabi* meant I also had to wear long sleeves and loose-fitting clothes—I was regularly policed on whether my clothes were loose enough for the "Islamic" space; this was ironic considering the building also housed other entities that were not identified as Islamic, as well as a cafeteria that was used by students and staff from all over Education City. Thus, all women in the building were not required to dress the way I was, but my role as a faculty member (and my non-Muslim and South Asian female body) required disciplining into an institutional identity that was defining itself directly against the "secular" and "Western" branch campuses.

As I moved between my office and classroom in the QFIS building, the building's cafeteria, and other spaces of research and teaching around the Education City campus, such as the other branch campus buildings and the HBKU student center, I would remove and re-don the hijab; I often chose clothing depending on which spaces I needed to occupy on a given day; I wore makeup on some days and not others; I dressed in casual or professional clothing depending on whom I was meeting; and I always made sure to have different layers of clothing with me to accommodate the various norms of the campus's spaces.

When I shared my experiences with my American branch campus colleagues, they were often shocked and asked me how I could tolerate such a "violation" of my rights. They then used my experiences as evidence of Qatari backwardness in conversations with others, folding them into the civilizational narratives that underpinned many of their understandings of the role of their universities in the Gulf and exceptionalist ideas of what constituted Qatari culture. These were the anthropological self/other binaries that my students and I were unpacking in the classroom and that critics of American university globalization relied on to challenge the existence of those classrooms. Nevertheless, I still had to think through what it meant to negotiate my bodily movements within Education City—at work, I was constantly policed by staff and faculty, yet my students were attuned to anticolonial politics in ways that exceeded those of students in American university classrooms, even those in branch campuses. In my Anthropology of the Middle East class, for example, they were quick to understand Edward Said's *Orientalism*, not only applying it to the Middle East and North Africa region but also using it to compare the contemporary experiences of Gazans with those of black Americans. I felt more comfortable in branch campuses because they resembled my academic home spaces in the United States; yet these were in many ways white spaces, where expertise mapped onto white bodies, and white colleagues practiced social segregation and often made disparaging comments about Qataris and other nationals, reminding me not only of how American liberal academia is racist but also of the traces of British and American colonial divisions that underpinned Gulf ethnoracial labor hierarchies (Amélie's chapter also discusses similar observations). My experiences of moving between spaces that increasingly embodied different epistemologies, gender norms, and social expectations highlighted not the failures of liberalism, as they did to the majority of my colleagues, but rather, I argue, revealed the archival nature of the American university, especially as it became more embedded within the local context.

Archiving Contestation

The post–civil rights US university has reassembled itself by archiving the oppositional social movements and alternate forms of knowledge of the 1960s–1980s in ways that depoliticize and contain difference (Ferguson 2012). The archival university labels and incorporates difference through the language of diversity, rendering it apolitical, digestible, and a metric of liberal success—part of the university's universal progress narrative. This is why it is not surprising for those of us who work in US universities to sometimes find ourselves in buildings where philosophy and women's studies, or classics and ethnic studies—disciplinary formations that are not just incommensurable but speak to one's historical annihilation of the other—are housed nicely together, sharing space and students, participating in projects of interdisciplinarity and global education, the buzzwords of today's university growth initiatives. At my current institution, I recall sitting on the International Affairs advisory committee and trying to explain to a room of mostly blank stares why a Europe concentration that included Greek and Roman mythology and traditional art history courses could not possibly fulfill the function of a global citizenship project; at the Texas A&M home campus, where I worked during a portion of this research project, I remember listening with my mouth open as the department of anthropology actively discussed, in all seriousness, a merger with classics: questions about how such a merger would fit with cultural anthropology's decolonial agenda, which included joint appointments in Africana studies and women's and gender studies, were dismissed or met with hostility. Such is the nature of the archival university.

I suggest that the postcolonial university is even more a site of archive than metropolitan institutions. We should indeed consider American branch campuses in Qatar postcolonial, in that they are part of a postcolonial state's attempts at building an indigenous education system, and in that the students they serve are Qatari or come from other postcolonial contexts. They are, of course, like most postcolonial sites, also spaces of ongoing and uneven imperial encounter. In 2014, my interlocutors were very concerned about what they read as a backlash against Education City by conservative elements of Qatari society, some of who were inside the new administrative scaffolding of HBKU. For my Western colleagues, attacks on coeducation in particular, which they saw as foundational to liberal education, and which many of them either implicitly or explicitly linked to their civilizational understandings of Qatari Muslim culture, signaled a major step backward in the gains they had made, and thus highlighted the fragility of the entire system of the branch campuses. I contend that this perceived backlash was instead an example of the Qatari-American university's capacity to archive oppositional politics. At the same time, examining the discourse of backlash opens up moments for questioning the moralities associated with liberal education's progress narratives; the outrage associated with my hijab dress code or rumors surrounding the Damien Hirst statue shroudings were less about producing a feminist campus, for example, than they were about reproducing an exceptionalized version of Qatari culture as both justification for liberal mission and scapegoat for liberal failure.

When I arrived in the fall of 2014 at the beginning of the school year to complete fieldwork for this project, Qatari women on a charity trip to the Amazon had just returned home after getting chastised on social media for not wearing their hijabs and for being photographed hiking with men. When a video of the coed trip, sponsored by Vodafone, went viral, the young women participants were denounced as shameful, their parents' child-rearing skills were called into question, and there was a slew of rather vicious personal attacks on individual team members that called into question their virtue and reputation, coming almost entirely from Qatari citizens (primarily men, but also some women). This incident caused concern among faculty and especially student affairs staff, at the branch campuses and at HBKU, about upcoming mixed-gender trips. A couple of trips had already been canceled or changed, in case of similar responses from community members. That year, an annual Halloween event, which included a haunted house cosponsored by Northwestern and Texas A&M, was not approved by HBKU administration. Halloween, apparently, was un-Islamic, and the haunted house would put men and women in too close proximity in a dark space to be respectable. Thus the event's name had been changed, the date had been moved from October 31 to the following week, and men and women would now enter the haunted house (which would no longer be referred to as haunted) separately. Other incidents I heard referred to as backlash were security guards enforcing curfews on the mixed-gender spaces of dorms, where no curfews were actually in place, and of Education City's new local reputation as Sin City, owing primarily to supposed transgressions on Qatari women's morality by mixing with men. One student at Northwestern even told me that her request to have a fund-raising (halal) hotdog-eating contest in 2013 was denied by the administration as inappropriate, although administrators would not openly claim that this was because of potential sexual connotations.

Faculty, staff, and students at branch campuses all related to me that policies and attitudes around heterosociality were increasingly unclear and more conservative since the inception of HBKU. While this was sometimes the case of branch campuses being proactively conservative, uncertainties around what counted as proper behavior usually occurred in the interstitial spaces between the branch campus buildings—those that were HBKU administered and therefore considered Qatari or local, and not American. Student housing, for example, was one site where these tensions played out, as student housing fell directly under HBKU administration. While men and women used to be housed in the same complex (though in different buildings and without access to each other's residence halls), the newly opened men's dormitories had essentially segregated residential life to opposite sides of campus. While geographically more difficult, the department of Residential Life still held mixed-gender events, and the social spaces and dining halls in the dorms were open to all members of the community, including staff and faculty. The security that patrolled the dorms, however, did not necessarily understand or conform to what public safety would look like on an American college campus, and often took a punitive rather than paternal approach to student behavior. Thus students would get arrested for things that would not normally warrant such action under the umbrella of American institutions, such as drinking or public displays of affection. This made international students, who populated the dorms, even more precarious, because if they were kicked out of housing or arrested, they were effectively no longer able to go to school because they could not afford to rent apartments in Doha. They might also face deportation.

I met with the head of Residential Life one morning in November 2014 to tour the new men's dormitories and ask about rumors of new curfew enforcement, especially around mixing. He told me that while there was ongoing conversation in his office about whether there ought to be a curfew, the incident of men getting kicked out of female dormitories that had sparked the rumors was due to one security officer's individual decision; it was not a new official policy. I asked how that could be: as vulnerable immigrant workers, security officers are probably not empowered to make such a decision. It would be hard for security guards on campus, who tended to be Filipino or Kenyan, to exercise authority over students. He told me that a Qatari manager had told officers to enforce curfews on men in women's dormitories. When such punitive actions took place, guards were usually following directives from higher management, who were mainly Qatari or Arab.

These narratives follow the idea that Qataris are resistant to gender integration. However, knowledge economy development in Qatar and the Gulf states fundamentally revolves around a form of state-sponsored feminism, in which the education of women and their entry into the workforce is explicitly centered, to the extent that women are surpassing men in tertiary education and make up the majority of matriculated students in many colleges and universities (Ridge 2014). Thus, there is nothing uniquely "Qatari" about homosociality, just as there is nothing uniquely liberal about coeducation, as the history of American college campuses, their historical exclusion of women, and the continuing legacy of American women's colleges show us.

The Academic Bridge Program (ABP), for example, is a local institution inside Education City that is coeducational, and it has met with almost no resistance from Qataris, even though most of the students at ABP come from gender-segregated public schools. ABP is a one-year program designed primarily for Qatari nationals to gain the skills they require to get into college, whether it be the national Qatar University, Education City schools, or schools abroad, although there are attendees from other nationalities, mostly Arabic-speaking.[7] ABP's curriculum and programming are designed to bolster basic skills, especially in English, but also to give men and women an opportunity to learn to work together in mixed environments through clubs, group work, gender-integrated classes, and social events. Activities at ABP are designed, according to administrators and faculty there that I spoke with, to "ease" students into coeducation while also helping them get into college. For example, they do not partner men and women right away for classwork; rather, they keep them separate for a bit and then slowly integrate them.

Alanoud, a Qatari staff member at ABP, explained that they were successful with Qataris because they created activities that were culturally appropriate. When planning activities, she explained, one should always ask what the aim is. Is it educational? The target should be to benefit the country, not to lose Qatari identity. As she emphasized, "Don't force them to be American!" The Academic Bridge Program, she said, focused much more on Muslim, Arab, and Qatari identity. She brought up Twitter complaints, for example, about how Georgetown had a large Christmas tree (we were meeting in December) but no *adhan* (call to prayer): "If you are preventing Islam, then why is there Christianity? Either have none, or all."[8] Alanoud reproduced state-sponsored feminism in our interview, noting that women were working harder and were more interested in education than ever, and that most of them were entering the workforce after graduation. However, her take on women's earnings was that they were disposable income, and that women were supported by men in their education and work aspirations. Women's education did not therefore include liberal feminist claims to rights and equality but rather was a part of constructing a patriarchal modern national femininity. A similar argument could be made for HBKU, which was shifting the structure of Education City and focusing in particular on creating an indigenous, non-Western university in Qatar, one that was able to include the branch campuses but did not model them.

Qatari families and HBKU middle managers did not seem to have the same anxieties about ABP that they had about the branch campuses, the dormitories, and certain Student Affairs events. This was particularly interesting since my colleagues at the branch campuses pinpointed heterosociality as the primary reason for Qatari backlash to the Education City project and for the lack of Qatari students joining in Student Affairs activities. The perceived threat of the mixed campus, then, was not about mixing itself, which is inevitable and already existing in many parts of Qatar, but about maintaining an imagined community of Qatariness that was founded on the myth of particular "traditional" Muslim gender roles—defined precisely against the presence of the non-Muslim, non-Arab expatriate as a threat to that tradition (see Chatterjee 1993; Longva 1997). This was why political opposition (read as backlash by my colleagues) and the concessions made to it manifested themselves on the bodies of Qatari women in particular; therefore, the pressures women felt to be "appropriate" were pervasive in the branch campuses in ways they were not in ABP. In addition, the critiques of Education City— through a discourse of gender threat—contained within them anti-imperial sentiments that were too readily dismissed as part of "conservative" or "backward" ideas about culture. This could explain the policing I experienced within the Faculty of Islamic Studies—as a particularly placed expatriate non-Muslim expert, but also as a South Asian brown-bodied woman who could be disciplined in certain ways but not in others (my pay and benefits, for example, were probably higher than those of many of my colleagues who did not hold American passports).

The changes in Education City were quite ordinary reflections of how institutions incorporate political contestations and calls for greater representation. Rather than producing a more fractured landscape of higher education, it is in these dissonant moments where we can see how archival logics were able to incorporate seemingly incommensurate political projects. The amalgam Qatari-American space of HBKU is not proof of the failure of liberal education in illiberal space, or evidence that globalizing the American university is an extension of crisis; rather, it is within the framework of liberalism's own logics. It offers a space of potential openings from which we can critique our categories of knowledge, especially around culture, and how culture is used within debates about global education, Gulf exceptionalism, and anthropology. American institutions are passing into places where they engage different publics, and in the process of their localization, the concept of education and its meanings are perhaps reconfigured.

Conclusion: Speaking Back

I was finishing this chapter and the larger book manuscript it references through the 2016 election cycle and the first few months of the Trump administration. During that time, I watched many of my colleagues and friends discuss the state of the United States on social media through parallels to Nazi Germany and fascism, or to African and Middle Eastern dictatorships, lamenting an end to liberal democracy, as if the roots of illiberalism were not planted in the very soil of the settler colonial racial states of the "New World," and the groundwork for Trump's nativist executive orders and domestic state terror were not laid by the Obama, Bush, and Clinton administrations. Natalie Koch (2017) has referred to this discourse as "Orientalizing authoritarianism," importing it from elsewhere in order to perpetuate US exceptionalism and illiberalism as exception, scripting Trump into accepted and knowable frameworks of imperial America, or what Chatterjee and Maira (2014) have referred to as "manifest knowledges."

I also witnessed a collective grief from white feminists after November 9, 2016 that sparked fissures and debates within academic and nonacademic feminist spaces about the absence of liberal feminism from activist movements like Black Lives Matter, No Dakota Access Pipeline (NoDAPL), and immigrant and Muslim rights struggles in the lead-up to the election— conversations and contestations that made "intersectionality" a concept that many more people are now thinking with in forming their political stakes. Watching the Women's March in its last days become a much more inclusive space that rippled globally, and then seeing taxi drivers strike at JFK and other airports while well-to-do lawyers scrambled to prepare motions and offer legal aid following Trump's "Muslim Ban," inspired hope in solidarity politics that pushed against identity and ideology, challenging many to move into previously unknown modes and vocabularies of mobilization and belonging. It is here in the known and unknown epistemologies of encounter, subjectification, and difference that I have always found this project and my role in it to reside; and this moment of American liberal crisis and imperial reinvigoration, while not at all exceptional, provides an interesting point of departure from Qatar and its branch campuses.

While academic/intellectual critiques of the American Left's response to Trump were well and good, embodied existence at my PWI (predominantly white institution), especially after students started becoming more and more frightened for themselves and their families, was a different thing. I began having temporary escape fantasies to the warmth and comfort of the Gulf, which started to solidify into questions about serious alternate academic possibilities for the first time in my career: what would it be like to work in a Gulf university, where my colleagues actually get paid livable wages, where they do not think of evenings and weekends as work time but instead enjoy leisure and family, where higher education is funded as a public good so they have the resources to take their students on trips to neighboring countries or to conferences, where I would have research funding and proximity to my field sites, where I would not always stand out demographically? I have explored some of these reasons for Muslim and nonwhite faculty taking jobs in the Gulf elsewhere (Vora 2018; see also Koch 2016).

I think it is not a small thing to highlight here that Dubai was the first city I ever lived in, as a PhD student in my thirties conducting dissertation research, where I woke up one day and realized that I had been moving through daily life without having to think about the brownness of my body, a feeling I had never felt before (see chapter 1). These cities, of course due in large part to my class privilege and my Western passport, but also because of their Muslimness and large South Asian populations, were for me spaces of cultural familiarity and relative gender safety in public space. There was deep comfort in Dubai and Doha—they were home spaces in ways that Pennsylvania, Texas, or most anywhere in the United States could never be—despite the different challenges and restrictions I faced there. And while we may be as academics rightfully suspicious of both the neocolonial and neoliberal aspects of the transnational American university, I think we have to be equally, if not more so, suspicious of what writing them off under grand narratives of neoliberalism and crisis recuperate and erase. For many of us, the answers to the violences of liberalism and democracy might not lie in the metropolitan American academy but in the elsewheres and in the imaginaries, intellectual communities, and home spaces, however fraught, that places like Education City offer.

The forms of belonging and exclusion taking place at universities in Qatar, as I hope I have begun to bring to life in this chapter, are diverse and vary between students, between classrooms, and between universities. It is impossible to paint them with one stroke just as it is impossible to paint metropolitan "home" institutions this way or to make the mistake of thinking that somewhere out there an idealized form of the university both exists and is potentially mobile. In my other work, for example, I trace how, for upwardly mobile local expats, university experiences were not simply about neoliberal consumption of educational services; rather, they increasingly included emerging liberal claims to civil rights and diasporic citizenship (Vora 2014a). And elsewhere, I explore how, for young Qatari women in my Texas A&M classroom, modernization brought new opportunities as well as reassertions of parochial understandings of who can claim rights to the country and its future (Vora 2015). The emerging identifications and interactions enabled by the American university may be changing the face of belonging in places like Doha while producing scholars who can engage the very debates within which they are imbricated.

Like postcolonial academics, who were also products of Western educational systems and significantly changed the landscape of the American academy in the 1980s and 1990s, these students have the potential to produce new approaches to questions of knowledge production, history, racialization, and power. The enormous activism across the Arab world that coincided with the span of this research project, along with the great devastation that the region has faced, represents young people in these countries questioning, challenging, and redefining state responsibility, freedom, citizenship, global power, and the very concept of the human. If the conversations many of us want to have about the state of higher education are rooted in questions about which practices, infrastructures, and institutions constitute public good, then youth in the Middle East at this moment are compulsory interlocutors. Shrouding their experiences behind "culture," especially through crude understandings of tradition and modernity, or dismissing these projects wholesale under a rubric of neoliberalism or imperialism, reproduces the exceptionalist discourses, colonial encounters, and anthropological forms of difference that the best forms of engaged ethnography and feminist scholarship have taught us to resist.

Notes

A version of this chapter was published as the conclusion of my book *Teach for Arabia* (2018).

1. The Qatar Foundation is the parastatal agency tasked with spearheading Qatar's "knowledge economy" development. It is responsible for overseeing all of the operations of the Education City complex, which contains several foreign university branch campuses, local institutions, K–12 schools, the Sidra hospital, and research centers, among others.

2. Of course, green projects as branding initiatives are not unique to the Gulf region.

3. Branch campuses operate on ten-year renewable contracts with the Qatar Foundation, whose parameters are similar to limited liability companies.

4. Since 2016, there has been further reorganization, and HBKU is now listed as a separate national graduate university inside Education City, partnered with the other international branch campuses. All student housing remains part of HBKU.

5. "Hamad bin Khalifa University reveals new brand identity," HBKU News, November 2, 2016, http://www.hbku.edu.qa/en/news/hamad-bin-khalifa-university-reveals -new-brand-identity.

6. QNRF is similar to the National Science Foundation (NSF) in the United States.

7. Qatar University switched most programs to Arabic in 2013, which resulted in the loss of many prospective QU students.

8. Georgetown is a Jesuit institution, so this might explain the Christmas tree, although Christmas trees are common in expatriate hotels and shopping malls in Qatar.

Chapter 4

CLASS STRUGGLE AND DE-EXCEPTIONALIZING THE GULF

AHMED KANNA

Let me begin this chapter by discussing societies that some have characterized as capitalist oligarchies because of their resistance to political liberalization as well as their hostility to universal suffrage and the legalization of trade unions. Well into the second century of their capitalist development, the employer classes of these societies depend on low-wage labor-intensive production. Unsurprisingly, this class opposes any liberalizing measures or laws that would empower workers, and they rely on violent labor repression to intimidate and discipline workers. Meanwhile, workers suffer under regimes of contract labor, similar to historical forms of bonded labor. Under the contract labor regime, the worker agrees to work for the employer for a stipulated amount of time, often, as the sociologist Vivek Chibber has written, for "several years, at a fixed rate of remuneration. Any attempt to renege on the bargain, either by quitting or by insisting on renegotiating the wage rate, [is] punishable by law. Employers [are] free to terminate the contract at any time, but workers lack . . . a symmetrical privilege. A worker who gain[s] employment under these terms . . . forfeit[s] the right to dispose of [their] labor power as [they wish]" (2013, 121). Moreover, employers could bring workers up on charges not only for quitting but also for unexcused absences (due to illness, for example) or for unsatisfactory performance. The bosses consider this to be "an encroachment on the employer's proprietary use of the employee's labor power" (121).

Every reader will know to which societies I am referring here because it is so obvious where these illiberal, indeed tyrannical, labor regimes exist. I am referring of course to England and the United States at the height of the Industrial Revolution. Or maybe the "obvious" referent lies somewhere else. For many contemporary writers, including not a few academics, this story of exploitation does not implicate the so-called liberal West.

The earlier chapters of the book addressed, through ethnographically detailed case studies, the ways that Orientalist and exceptionalizing discourses produced in imperial and capitalist geopolitical contexts reduced the complexity of societies in the Arab Gulf and Arabian Peninsula and continue to play into ongoing projects of militarism and capitalist accumulation in the region. This chapter seeks to complement the discursive and postcolonial critique of the earlier ones by bringing a class-struggle perspective to the question of labor exploitation in the region, an interpretive frame based on my extensive reading of the literature on a variety of Gulf countries combined with my own ethnographic work in Dubai in particular. In this chapter I focus on a particular figure, that of the foreign worker. My argument is that both liberal and neocolonial Western representations of the working-class migrant have been central to these exceptionalizing discourses. In the popular imagination of many in the Global North/West, the Gulf is almost automatically associated with hyperexploited, abused workers, primarily from South Asia. As I show in this chapter, while these discourses are not entirely a fabrication—massive exploitation based on the racialization and patriarchal gendering of labor in the Gulf is very real—there is at the same time a disavowal in these Orientalist discourses that is either duplicitous or naive, an echo of the "Orientalizing [of] authoritarianism" discussed in the previous chapter (see Koch 2017). Seen from a feminist and Marxist class-struggle perspective, the racialized exploitation of foreign workers is perhaps the aspect of Gulf societies that is *most* similar to the neoliberal societies of the North. The Gulf is least exceptional with respect to its regimes of labor exploitation.

In this chapter I apply a feminist and Marxist political and analytical framework to two areas in particular. First, this framework highlights patterns across and beyond the Gulf region, allowing a better grasp of class dynamics that transcend national boundaries. Such dynamics are not sufficiently addressed by perspectives that eschew Marxist concepts such as labor exploitation, surplus value, and production and social reproduction. While the research discussed in the introduction of this book has moved Arabian Peninsula scholarship in innovative directions, grappling more complexly than before with questions of urbanity, sociopolitics, disciplinary and biopolitical subject formation, and the politics of infrastructure and technopolitics, processes of class struggle and exploitation have been less emphasized as focal points of research agendas. When class struggle does appear, it is often seen through the frameworks of human rights or narratives of worker victimhood.

While it might be obvious to state, for many, perhaps most of the residents of the UAE, Qatar, and to a significant though lesser extent, Bahrain, Kuwait, and Saudi Arabia, the region is primarily a destination for and space of work. In interviews and conversations I conducted with members of the diverse, mostly noncitizen Dubai working class during the research for my first book, labor figured prominently in interlocutors' discussions of their experiences (Kanna 2011). For both workers involved primarily in the arena of production and others who labored mainly in social reproduction, the labor process and spaces of labor circumscribed and dominated their lives. If one side of modernity in GCC countries is the "image of unlimited good" and ostensible "realm of freedom" from economic necessity supposedly provided by the oil age, then the other side is the tyranny of economic necessity, the "silent compulsion of economic relations" as Karl Marx (1976, 899) put it.[1] With respect to the latter, life in Arabian Peninsula societies since the discovery of oil can only be understood by reference to, and is a complex effect of, processes of accumulation by dispossession characterizing the wider Global South under neoliberalism (Federici 2010; Harvey 2005, 2014).

In the first chapter we discussed how Western, in particular British, American, and French, notions of race intersected with local Arab hierarchies and national state projects of labor hierarchy to racialize labor in specific ways. As Robert Vitalis (2007) has shown in the case of Saudi Arabia, the logic of American Jim Crow racism was central to the creation and shaping not only of the Arabian oil frontier but also of the modern Saudi state's ethnopolitics. As I have discussed in my work on Dubai leisure spaces in the early twenty-first century, racialized logics of bourgeois comfort and mappings of urban space were the legacy of long histories of British and American intervention in the region (Kanna 2014). Colonial logics of whiteness and masculinity informed hierarchies of desirable and undesirable labor, remuneration, and spatial segregation of work and leisure spaces, and in turn reproduced simplified categories applied to workers who were identified as non-European. Simultaneously, labor was also gendered. In the case of Dubai, where I conducted almost two years of fieldwork, ascribed cis/het gender categories confront any observer with the sheer starkness of their binary logic. The foreign working class is both far more surveilled and far more gender segregated than are middle- and upper-class foreigners. Unlike the latter, for example, working-class foreigners are rarely, if ever, allowed to bring their families (though of course this is not to imply that working-class foreigners are more likely than others to be involved in or to desire heteronormative relations or family structures). Working-class foreigners are individuated and spatially gender segregated in stark ways, forms of spatial and ascriptive identification that are distinct from but through which the related process of individual identity formation must inevitably pass. In this sense, unlike chapter 1's emphasis on what might be called *identity*, the process of self-formation seen from the perspective of the individual subject, this chapter's focus is on the political-economic dynamics of what Fields and Fields (2012) have called *identification*, the extra-subjective (or, if one likes, objective) structures that are an important factor in the shaping of identity.

Vitalis (2007) calls the modern oil-industrial order taking shape in Saudi Arabia the regime that race built. This is true. But race and racialization are not the only or the fundamental impetus in the production of Arab Gulf modernity and urban spatiality. They intersect with gender and class and are unified in the project of capital everywhere: ensuring a divided and weak working class. Against a race-only or race-as-motivating-factor approach, Barbara Fields (1990) famously points out that the purpose, for example, of American slavery was not the production of white supremacy but rather of profits. Similarly, the exporting of Jim Crow conditions to the Aramco oil fields, or "ethnocracy" more broadly, is not the goal of capital in the Gulf, though they are of course important vehicles for ensuring hyperexploitation (Hanieh 2011).

The feminist scholar and activist Silvia Federici has questioned the assumption that Marx and many other Marxists have made, that capitalism is historically revolutionary (Federici 2004). In the orthodox (i.e., male-centered version), the story goes like this: in being robbed of their means of production, medieval peasants were nevertheless "liberated" of traditional feudal bonds and became "free" labor. In depriving peasants of some modicum of control over their subsistence, the capitalist hand that took also gave: the expropriated peasant was now able to sell his labor on the market. The "his," in orthodox Marxism, is gender blind, applying, supposedly, to all labor. But as Federici points out, it was male labor, in general, that went to market to self-commodify. Capitalism's emergence and its deprivation of female access to the common (gardens, fields, etc.) tended to have a different and gendered effect on females; indeed, capitalism produced gender in new and more binary ways. Capitalist transformation in early modern Europe, for example, incarcerated women in their homes and in their bodies and deprived them of the ability to sell their labor on the market as "free labor."

The generalization of free labor to all labor is erroneous, writes Federici (2004), and the error is a trick of the gender blindness shared by many Marxists and non-Marxists alike. Both in its European birthplace and as it was transported by European empires to non-European lands, capitalism destroyed women's power and intensified masculine power simultaneously and dialectically. In cutting off most of humanity from control over its means of production, it also masculinized public space, in turn conditioning an increasingly binary and arbitrary division between (paid) "production" and (unpaid) "social reproduction." Further, the body came increasingly to define and constitute femininity. The body of women under capitalism became what the factory became for male wage workers: the primary ground for exploitation—and resistance (Federici 2004, 15–16, 22).

This perspective allows us to form a compelling picture of the "factory-like" conditions of twenty-first-century capitalist exploitation in the Gulf, in terms of what Marx (1976) refers to as the production of surplus value and to social reproduction, what the feminist and Marxist Nancy Fraser (2014) has called the "back-story" to Marx's "hidden abode" of production. A case such as Dubai presents a form of capitalism characterized by a more binary gendering and more binary production: social reproduction division, all of which is racialized under colonial logics of whiteness.[2] Far from being the expression of a cultural logic, these are formed at the intersection of transnational and local capitalist class projects with roots in colonialism. Both kinds of labor—that which is gendered as male and that which is gendered as female, both racialized as non-European—are the basic condition of possibility for the kinds of bourgeois and racist notions of space and bodily comfort discussed in previous chapters. Construction site, domestic space, leisure space: all become arenas for the spatial production of the order that race and also gender and class has built.

This part of West and South Asia has tended to be seen as the exception to processes more clearly recognized as capitalist accumulation in other parts of the world. This is the second reason that recommends feminist Marxist theory as an analytical framework. Whether in a more classical Orientalist vein or promoting narratives of the "hyper-modern" Gulf (see Kanna 2011, 77–104), mass media and even academic representations have tended to frame the region as exceptional, with its social, political, and urban forms a result of a supposedly underlying, unchanging cultural identity. One of the tropes that have perpetuated this notion of an exceptional Gulf has been representations of the foreign worker from South Asia. It is this figure on which Western liberal discourses have most often relied in constructing their image of the exceptional Arabian Peninsula, where both male and female workers are, supposedly, uniquely exploited. Campaigns by Western liberals advocating divestment of American universities from Gulf satellite campuses, for example, often traffic in the term "slavery" to describe South Asian workers in the Gulf; the pages of left-liberal websites and mainstream media do the same. These discourses do not even pretend, most of the time, to distance themselves from the "bad old" Orientalism.

A Conversation at a Worker Housing Compound

Writing on Dubai, the geographer Michelle Buckley claims, correctly, that

> Dubai occupies a somewhat contradictory place within debates on neoliberalism. On one hand, the corporatized logics of governance that operate in the city are used to justify portrayals of the city as a "deviant" state . . . whose urban process and social inequalities are understood primarily in relation to their marked divergence from the civic traditions and class compromises of liberal democratic cities of the West. On the other hand, however, these constructions of Dubai also portray the city as a kind of political economic simulacrum, its autocratic free-marketeering a truer expression of neoliberalism, in some sense, than the Western heartlands from which it emerged. (2013, 261)

Buckley's essay on Dubai neoliberalism addresses some of the basic problems of the dominant critical discourse on Gulf neoliberalism (Ali 2010; Davis 2006; Davis and Monk 2007; Harvey 2008). She correctly rejects as teleological and totalizing those narratives of Dubai as "pure neoliberalism," of Gulf neoliberalism as uncontested, and of workers as a voiceless homogeneous mass lacking agency. We need, she argues, to "decouple[e] understandings of neoliberalized labour relations from post-Fordist-inspired storylines about the erosion of formal, Keynesian labour power" and to see Dubai's neoliberalism as a "hybridized" form combining aspects of neoliberalism as it exists in the countries of the North with elements of dynastic state authoritarianism (Buckley 2013, 270). Yet, what is remarkable about Buckley's account of Dubai is how *unremarkable* the city's class structure comes to appear, how unsurprising its class relations are, from a Marxist perspective. Most of the ethnographic material presented by Buckley, which I discuss in more detail below, relates to the struggle by Dubai construction workers to be paid a living wage, to improve their housing, and to have their contracts respected; and also with the capitalist class's attempts to use the state to retaliate against those workers.

It was during a visit I made to one of Dubai's main worker housing compounds, what in the popular media are called "labor camps," that workers' understanding of how unremarkable Dubai was first became clear to me in a concrete way.[3] During early 2007, I visited a compound in the northeastern part of the city, past the airport and well outside the flashy newer neighborhoods that professional middle-class visitors usually encounter. A journalist friend of mine who writes on labor issues had put me in touch with a guide, a local labor activist and fixer, who offered to introduce me to some construction workers. We set out a few days after we first met at a hotel café for introductions and to discuss logistics.

"Shall we take my car or yours?" I ask him.

"Are your windows tinted?" he says. They are not. "Better take mine then," he replies. It has "100% tinting [on the windows]. It used to have 150%, but it was too dark." The 100 percent windows are still very dark. "If you try to look inside [the car] you will only see your face [reflected back at you]." His ominous tone adds a hint of menace to the proceedings, and, I later realize, it frames how I would go on to think about this incident for years.

I ask him to tell me more about the security situation at the housing complex that we are about to visit.

"Each company has its own security. I have a good relationship with the security man at this site. If the government catches us, we will both be screwed."

We drive about ten to fifteen minutes east of the Dubai neighborhood of Deira. Eventually we turn off the paved roads and onto unpaved ones. Walking along the sides of the road are long lines of men in the uniforms of different construction companies, returning from or going to their shifts. Groups of men exit buses and are replaced by others. We pass a couple of residential compounds.

"That one is al-Habtoor. That is DPFC," says my guide, naming two prominent companies and pointing to the camp walls and buses emblazoned with the respective company's logos. "That one is Al Abbar," owned by one of Dubai's most prominent business families, one of whose members is a top government official. These are all big companies, with uncooperative security personnel, he says, and with strict, brutal surveillance of their workers. They are too dangerous to attempt entry. We turn off and reach our destination.

The guard at the residence compound we go to is not even at the security kiosk. We proceed into a walled compound, past some communal bathrooms. There are six or seven bedrooms on either side of the compound, a common kitchen, and a TV area with easy chairs and sofas. The guide leads me into one of the bedrooms.

The room, which has two single and two bunk beds, is about forty square feet. It has its own kitchen and toilet. I am surprised to find a TV connected to a satellite dish and a stereo box. What are "victimized" workers doing with such "luxuries," I remember thinking at the time. We are greeted warmly by an Arab worker. He offers us tea, and he and the guide make small talk, the guide telling him that I am in the country to research the lives of workers, what their experiences working in the UAE are. My guide turns and says to me, "This is a very good room," relative to other worker accommodations both at this company and at others. "Usually, a room like this houses twenty workers."

This worker, who comes from Egypt, has been in Dubai a little over three years. He found out about the job from an agent in his home country. For Dh 2,400 (about $650), he obtained a visa and airfare. The company paid for the remaining expenses, such as his health card and accommodations. Every three years he is required to renew the visa, at a rate of Dh 950. Every two years he gets two months' paid vacation, and the company allows trips home for emergencies. The company took his passport, but gives it back to him when he needs to travel. His monthly salary is Dh 1,100, always paid in cash. Sometimes he does not get paid for one or two months, sometimes more.

The sponsor, or *kafeel*, he tells me, is a small construction company with about twenty-five or thirty workers and described by the guide and the workers as a relatively "good" company.

What does he want to get out of Dubai? I ask him.

"I don't have a big, definite goal. I dream step by step [*ahlam daraja fi daraja*]." He does not know how long he wants to stay in Dubai. He is here indefinitely.

We move on to a common area, where about a dozen workers are hanging out. They are from Pakistan, they tell me, and one of them, a thirtysomething man wearing a *shalwar qameez*, tells me about his experience. He found this job through an agency in Islamabad. He paid for his own airfare and visa, at a total of Rs (PK) 130,000 (just under $1,100). When he arrived in Dubai, the company took his passport and a Dh 1,000 deposit, which the employer called *ta'min*, or insurance. What does it insure against? That he does not "abscond" as the employers say. Like the Egyptian worker we spoke to earlier, he receives two months' vacation and emergency travel home. His monthly salary is Dh 600 (just over half of what the Egyptian worker makes), and he works about forty-eight hours, plus about two to three hours of overtime, every week, which increases his income to about Dh 800. Whereas the government requires that the sponsor pay for accommodations and electricity (and this company does seem to follow the rules), he must pay for food and cooking gas himself, which leaves Dh 500 net. All of this goes to his family in Pakistan.

There is a canteen at the camp, or "company accommodation," to use the bosses' term. "But it is very expensive," says the Egyptian worker. It is more expensive than Spinney's or Carrefour, says my guide, referring to two fancy Western supermarkets frequented by Dubai's middle and upper-middle classes. "If a carton of milk costs Dh 3 at Spinney's, it will cost Dh 3.50 here. But the workers have no choice. The canteen has a monopoly."

"This is actually a pretty good company," says the guide.

There is a much worse one, the East Coast and Hamriya, in Sharjah. At this company, the workers sleep on the roofs. There is no plumbing, no electricity, no food, no work. The workers are all "illegal." The sponsor has not returned their passports for two years. There are about thirty-five workers. The sponsor owes them about Dh 250,000. About ten of them went to their embassies to get replacement papers and have left the UAE. The partners were an Emirati sheikh and a Lebanese Canadian. They dumped the company when it went bankrupt, and left their workers hanging out to dry.

The third worker to whom we speak is an elderly Pakistani. He has been with the company for over fifteen years. It cost him about Rs (PK) 150,000 to get to the UAE, but some workers, he says, pay Rs 200,000. "The agencies lie. They say 'go to Dubai, the work is easy, the life is easy, you will do light work like lifting crates. Small work, little work.' The agent is too much [*sic*] bastard." Workers from Pakistan, he says, cannot read either Arabic or English, but they are forced to sign contracts in those languages. This allows companies to evade responsibility when workers make complaints. "The Dubai government is good," better than the Pakistan government; it cares more about workers, he claims. "But the companies are not good."

Marxist Analysis and De-exceptionalizing the Gulf

When I think back on this encounter with Dubai construction workers, I am struck first of all by the way I had enveloped it, for years after it occurred, in an atmosphere of menace. At around the time of my visit to the residence compound, Human Rights Watch (2006) had published one of its periodic reports on abuses and deaths of workers in the UAE. When I arrived in the field in late 2006, the report was definitely on people's minds. My Emirati interlocutors tended to minimize or even deny that abuses existed. One, a well-to-do business student, said such reports took a lot out of context. He was clearly just shrugging his shoulders. Another, a middle-aged sociologist with close ties to the ruling family in Abu Dhabi, dismissed such reports as the work of the CIA. A third, a young manager at a large Dubai corporation, denied the legitimacy of even raising the issue, saying to me rhetorically: "A country is like a company, they both have to make a profit." By contrast, my Indian interlocutors believed these reports to be true, some expressing the sentiment that "finally" some light had been shone on the reality of what was being done to foreign workers.

As valuable as such human rights work is in shedding light on labor exploitation and abuses, and as much as I agree with my Indian over my

Emirati interlocutors on this issue, the way in which human rights discourse traffics in images of worker victimization has tended to miss the complexity of class relations in the UAE. Human rights discourse also produces and reproduces liberal logics of labor exploitation as a moral issue, one where exploitation issues from the moral character of those in power rather than from a class structure that positions individuals in ways that strongly influence their choices. The conversations I had with workers, in which they expressed their matter-of-fact attitude to work in Dubai, capture this structural aspect of exploitation that is missed by a human rights perspective.

In retrospect, what I was searching for in going to the worker housing compound was something like a smoking gun, a "truth behind" the narrative of the gleaming *Mithal Dubai* (The Dubai model). I was unconsciously trying to write a story that would merely confirm prejudices I had had in my mind from various sources, from Orientalist depictions of "evil Arabs," to, paradoxically, self-Orientalizing ideas about "good," "civilized" Arabs (see chapter 1), to human rights organizations' moral discourses. What I found instead was something more complicated that I did not recognize at the time: workers leading blasé everyday lives and talking about work from the vantage point not of victims but of pragmatic actors navigating lives that were exploitative but that, as they told it, could have been worse. This is not to deny that other workers were treated much worse. Indeed, the Human Rights Watch reports produced out of the UAE are valuable for the truths they unearth and the abuses they attempt to remedy. But this case shows that there are other workers who, though they are not experiencing the most predatory and brutal forms of class oppression in the UAE, are nevertheless struggling with capitalist exploitation. They are not being left to rot on the roofs of a residential compound abandoned by the boss. But they are taking home $150 a month in one of the most expensive cities in the Middle East, if not the world. They are dealing with hyperexploitation layered atop the dispossession to which they are subjected by labor agents. Though their accommodations and the few "benefits" they earn (vacations, for example) make their lives more tolerable than those experienced by even more exploited workers, they still live under constant surveillance and threat of physical coercion by goonish security men hired by the boss. This intersection of wage exploitation, accumulation by dispossession, and physical coercion, as I discuss in the concluding remarks to this chapter, is in fact typical of societies under capitalism. It is in no way unique to Dubai, the Gulf, or the Arabian Peninsula.

The experiences and the testimonies of the workers whom I just discussed highlight a fact that would be obvious were it not for the obfuscatory effect of exceptionalizing discourses: that the Gulf is a region of near-constant capital versus labor struggle. This has been a fact since the colonial era, the result of a capitalist class structure focused with laser-like intensity on the production of what Marx (1976) called absolute surplus value in key sectors, such as construction.[4] Moreover, as I discuss in further detail below, the migrant labor class relation and its intensification of the rate of labor exploitation are similar, if not in many ways identical, to that prevailing in the countries of the "liberal" North (Lewis et al. 2015; Ollus 2016).

In the arenas of both production and social reproduction, processes of racialization and gendering intersect to produce labor hyperexploitation. It is my contention in this chapter that not only can we *not* contrast the "liberal" North and the "illiberal" Gulf in any binary way; we must also point to the fact that capital often employs the very same tactics of labor coercion and discipline in both cases, with both so-called liberal states of the North and the supposedly illiberal states of the Gulf employing similar practices and policies of labor discipline and partaking in broader discourses of labor "othering."

Looking at the spheres of production and social reproduction from a class-struggle perspective, this chapter attempts to answer some key questions: To what extent can we use capital—in the Marxist sense—as an explanatory category to understand how power works in a postcolonial context, in other words, those outside the classical heartlands of capitalism? In what ways, moreover, is the accumulation of surplus value in the Gulf continuous with, and in what ways does it depart from, the wider history of capitalism? What, as Vivek Chibber (2013) has put it, does capital universalize, and, if it makes sense to see at least some fundamental aspects of capital as universal, in what ways can we apply this insight to the question of Gulf exceptionalism? Approaching the issue of Gulf exceptionalism in this way, we can more clearly see how the figures that are assumed to mark the Gulf as most exceptional— those of the supposedly voiceless and helpless foreign laborer, and by extension, the supposedly exceptional capital-labor relation in the Gulf—in fact indicate the ways in which the Gulf *is least exceptional*.

I would go even further. A promising trend in labor scholarship has begun focusing on migrant labor, especially in the countries of the Global North. This work sees migrant labor, correctly, as central to both surplus value production and social reproduction in the capitalist North. Some scholars within this field have proposed the category of "hyperprecarity" in order to understand labor processes under neoliberal regimes. As an important contribution argues, the concept of hyperprecarity is meant both to highlight the differences between various kinds of exploitation under these regimes and at the same time to focus attention on the basic structure of exploitation that cuts across them. Yet one nevertheless gets the sense that many scholars see this condition of hyperprecarity as something new, as coeval with neoliberalism (Lewis et al. 2015, 584). Expanding our frame of analysis beyond the Global North to bring in regions such as the Gulf shows that hyperprecarity actually precedes and does not even necessarily presuppose neoliberalism. In the Gulf, what these scholars have called hyperprecarity came at the time of the construction of the national-migrant binary and the consequent creation and arrangement of different demographic groups into a labor "hierarchy of desirability" (583). This happened under decidedly non-neoliberal—one might even say state—developmentalist conditions. In Kuwait, for example, the process of constructing the national-migrant binary began in the 1950s, and in Saudi Arabia it began in the early 1960s (Hanieh 2011, 60–62). The same occurred later in the UAE and Qatar. In all cases, this state-bureaucratic production of the "migrant" and of hierarchies of (un)desirable labor took place in the context of increased anticolonial and often anticapitalist labor militancy. In short, hyperprecarity emerged in the Gulf earlier than in the neoliberal North, and was the result of a great deal more state intervention than is normally associated with neoliberalism.[5]

Gendered Hyperexploitation: Historical and Contemporary Cases

As the geographer Adam Hanieh (2011, 54) writes, the "centrality of the Gulf to the structure of the global economy means that the working classes of the Gulf (and, by extension, the Middle East) present a significant potential threat to capital accumulation at a global scale." This "partially explains the peculiar character of working class formation in the GCC—overwhelmingly constituted by temporary, migrant workers with no citizenship rights. Class formation in the Gulf has occurred through its spatial structuring, and this feature is linked to the role the region plays in the global economy" (54). While we acknowledge this peculiarity, the historical and contemporary anthropological evidence cautions against the temptation to exaggerate this.

For example, why not include the region in a global history of labor uprisings? To include the Gulf (if not the wider Arabian Peninsula) in the usual leftist framework of "revolutionary rehearsals" (Chile, Prague Spring, the global '68, etc.) might seem absurd, but that really says more about the lacunae of dominant frameworks than it does about the supposed absurdity of the referent. After all, this part of Western Asia is and has been very much like other mineral extraction and strategic chokepoint zones, a place of intense labor conflict with capital and the state (Chalcraft 2011; Davidson 2008; Menoret 2014; Vitalis 2007; Wright 2015).[6] With respect to the Gulf in particular, labor history in the region reveals a pattern of increasing labor militancy leading to the creation of national identity categories and boundaries through which the Gulf capitalist class has sought to divide labor into national and foreign layers. This is not a simple top-down divide-and-rule story, however, but rather a dialectical process of hegemony and identity formation. As John Chalcraft (2011) has shown, for example, the seeds of Arab nationalism were always present in the labor and anticolonial movements in the region. By the mid-twentieth century, the Gulf ruling class began appropriating Arab nationalism both to reproduce and to intensify emerging hierarchies of labor desirability and relative precarity.

As historians such as Chalcraft have shown, workers, students, and sometimes the professional middle classes agitated, went on strike, and demanded reforms throughout the period of the 1920s–1950s. The most dramatic of these movements occurred in Saudi Arabia between March 1953 and June 1956, a time widely regarded as the most important round of Aramco mobilizations. These mobilizations featured petitions, demonstrations, strikes, and boycotts and threatened to develop into an organized workers movement. "Thousands of workers—most of the Aramco workforce— appear to have participated," writes Chalcraft. As with previous movements in Bahrain, Kuwait, and Saudi Arabia, this movement combined calls for increased economic rights, worker power, and anticolonialism. The workers rejected low pay, poor working conditions, and the racism of American and Saudi bosses and called for the "right to elect worker representatives, an end to discrimination against the Shi'a, a more equitable distribution of oil revenues, and closing the American air force base in Dhahran" (Chalcraft 2011, 38). Agitation by Saudi workers continued well into the 1960s and occurred elsewhere in the region. Often these protests were interwoven with Arab nationalist sentiments and were led by organizers who were oriented to that form of politics, although the aforementioned Aramco workers movement in embryo tended in a more socialist direction. Either way, both the imperial British and American states and their local comprador indigenous rulers—an "axis of reaction" one might call it—viewed any such agitation with deep hostility.

It is therefore neither an accident nor surprising that, by this time, the Gulf states responded not only with repression but also, notes Hanieh, with a "particular *spatial strategy*," an increasing reliance on temporary migrant labor tied to an extremely narrow definition of citizenship (2011, 59–60).[7] Attempts by workers to resist or protest working conditions posed a threat not only to local elites but also, it is no exaggeration to say, to the global capitalist order given how central Gulf labor is to reproducing one of the core zones of postwar imperialism. As Hanieh notes, Gulf worker militancy presaged "the emergence of a potential link between the control of oil (and its revenues), and the ability to use this control to reshape the politics of the region as a whole—moving it out of the ambit of US power or the capitalist world market" (2011, 60–61).

It was during this high point of labor militancy in the 1950s and 1960s that the Gulf states deployed the "spatial fix" (as Hanieh puts it) that would ensure pacific conditions of profit accumulation and, in turn, financialization on a global scale. That spatial fix was the concept of citizenship based on Arab ethnicity or *asl*, and its mapping, in turn, onto the higher reaches of the hierarchy of labor desirability. This can be seen spatially in the Aramco labor camps, segregated along racial lines (Vitalis 2007), and temporally, most clearly, in the following numbers. In 1958, Saudi nationals constituted over 70 percent of Aramco's workforce, and in the early 1960s, they constituted over 90 percent of the workforce in Saudi Arabia. By 1980, migrant labor made up the majority of the Saudi workforce (50.7 percent). In Kuwait, a series of laws issued in the 1950s and 1960s deliberately aimed to differentiate Kuwaiti and expatriate labor. Across the region, writes Hanieh, "class congealed spatially around temporary migrant labor flows and was demarcated through the institution of citizenship" (2011, 61–63).

This spatial fix functioned in a number of ways to intensify profit accumulation.[8] The structural reliance on temporary migrant labor increased the rate of exploitation such that in Dubai, for example, construction workers earn between fifty and eighty cents per hour, working ten-hour days, six days a week, living under rent and housing regimes that further entangle them in already hyperexploitative relations of debt, a condition that clearly can be described as a form of hyperprecarity. What in Marxist terms is the reserve army of Middle Eastern and Asian labor is externalized outside the Gulf states, with the region relying on surrounding states to supply cheap labor. Also, the spatialization of class occurs "between spatially distinct sets of social relations" acting to depress the price of labor power; this form of spatialization acts as a powerful kind of social control. Migrant labor in the Gulf, in other words, lacks a "permanent right to space," is under constant threat of deportation, and is subject to illegality at the end of labor contracts, or even based on arbitrary shortening of contracts (Hanieh 2011, 64–65).

So far the workers that have been discussed, both in my ethnographic example from the workers' residence compound and in the literature (Chalcraft 2011; Hanieh 2011; Vitalis 2007), have been men. What about women workers? Because there are gendered obstacles to women's labor organizing that are not present in the case of male workers, which are related both to specific local conditions and to larger patterns of gendered work under capitalism, it might seem that stories of women workers' agency and even militancy are absent from the larger narrative of class struggle in the region. This would be another myth.[9]

While it is important to note that foreign women workers work in many occupations, from the service sector to social reproduction, the main sector in which foreign female workers are employed in the Gulf is domestic labor. This is in contrast to other Arab countries, such as Egypt, which has historically employed significant numbers of women in industrial production (Hammad 2016). Finding statistics, let alone establishing their credibility, is notoriously difficult with respect to foreign workers in the Gulf. One typical NGO, Migrant Rights, publishes a useful website that, if read alongside materials such as Human Rights Watch reports, which have better citation and data sourcing, paint an overall picture in which the vast bulk of social reproduction labor in the region is done by foreign women workers.[10] Excluded from the protections (minimal as they are) offered under the GCC countries' national labor laws, they suffer abuses such as "unpaid wages, confinement to the house, workdays of up to twenty-one hours with no rest and no days off, and in some cases, physical or sexual assault by employers. Domestic workers face legal and practical obstacles to redress, and many return home without justice" (Human Rights Watch 2014).

As Marxist and socialist feminists such as Margaret Benston (2019[1969]), Silvia Federici (2004, 2010, 2019), Lise Vogel (2013, 2019), Johanna Brenner (2017), and Tithi Bhattacharya (2015), among others, have long argued, the work of social reproduction under capitalism has been an arena of mostly unpaid, or at best underpaid, labor done mostly by women. This has a double significance for the capitalist mode of production. Female social reproduction labor not only adds a significant share to the freely appropriated value inherent to wage exploitation, it also, more importantly, reproduces labor power, and thus is as structurally fundamental to the capitalist mode of production as wage exploitation. Whether children are raised to adulthood in the society where they enter the labor force, or whether they arrive as foreign adults, their education, feeding, care, and so forth have generally been done by unpaid women. For capitalists, this is a rip-off even more massive than that which they extract from surplus labor in the workplace (Brown 2019).[11]

The anthropologist and scholar of Gulf migration Pardis Mahdavi has applied some of these key insights to the Gulf. In particular, she has looked at work done by women in the Gulf from the perspective of structural violence, which she argues is built into the policies of Gulf states. These are policies whereby the work of social reproduction and sex work are categorized by the state as distinct from surplus value production and privatized within the domestic sphere, into which the state almost never intervenes on behalf of workers (Mahdavi 2013). Furthermore, female workers experience obstacles to their organizing that male workers usually do not. The kafala system bonds both male and female workers to their employer, permitting workers, for example, to change jobs only with their employer's consent and allowing employers to terminate sponsorship, and therefore the right to legal residence in the UAE, at will. Unlike other categories of workers, domestic workers and sex workers are excluded entirely from labor law protections such as limits on working hours and overtime pay.[12] Any attempt to secure another job not authorized by the employer casts the domestic worker into a status of illegality. Systems of gendered structural violence render the boundary between legality and illegality porous and mean that some women workers choose the latter as a more secure form of employment (see De Regt 2010). As Mahdavi points out, for example, some women workers turn to sex work to ameliorate or escape from hyperexploitative domestic work, in spite of the higher risk of exposure to moral panics over "threats to national or Islamic identity" posed by sex work, from the perspectives of the heteronormative patriarchal state and dominant national discourses (Mahdavi 2013; see also Longva 1997).

While scholars such as Buckley (2013) and others (Davidson 2008; Kanna 2011) have highlighted the forms of resistance, such as mass strikes, engaged in by male construction workers, female social reproduction workers have also engaged in organized resistance. Women domestic workers, for example, have mobilized against the worst of the abuses to which they are subjected, such as transnational volunteer associations and migrant alliance networks (Johnson and Wilcke 2015). In the case of some nationalities, such as with Philippine nationals in Saudi Arabia, workers can rely on compatriots whose class position or higher income level offers them more security and who can provide support for workers who choose to leave undesirable jobs (Johnson and Wilcke 2015). Which brings us to the most common means by which women workers can escape abusive or excessively exploitative work: what the bosses term "absconding" and what workers term "freelancing." This means, simply, walking off the job and looking for a better one (Johnson and Wilcke 2015). While this does carry major risks, such as illegalization and, relatedly, a heightened vulnerability to the Gulf's "deportation regime" (De Genova and Peutz 2010), scholars have shown how in many cases workers who freelance have improved their pay and working conditions (Mahdavi 2013; Johnson and Wilcke 2015). As Mahdavi has written, freelancing and, in some cases, abandoning domestic work for sex work shows that "migrant women are not wholly victims of circumstance and can exercise agency in various ways. They demonstrate this through the decisions they make and the ways in which they navigate their experiences as migrant workers in the UAE" (2013, 437).

In recent years, scholars of migrant labor have begun using the term "hyperprecarity" to describe the condition of foreign workers suffering multiple intersecting structural vulnerabilities, from noncitizen and often undocumented status to racialization to gender hierarchy. Focusing on the Global North, this literature has tended to argue that hyperprecarity is roughly coterminous with the period of neoliberalism. However, a Gulf de-exceptionalization perspective suggests that hypreprecarity is neither exclusive to North or South nor is it necessarily a neoliberal phenomenon.

On Hyperprecarity, North and South

As the work of numerous scholars has shown, various forms of labor resistance, protests, and militancy against the Gulf countries' capitalist order and class structure are pervasive even today (Buckley 2013; Davidson 2008; Johnson and Wilcke 2015; Kanna 2011; Mahdavi 2011, 2013; Menoret 2014). The work of the geographer Michelle Buckley on Dubai has been especially clear and eloquent on this topic. She notes that during "the mid 2000s, dozens of highly public strikes by migrant construction workers swept across Dubai" (Buckley 2013, 265). Moreover, dozens of labor actions such as strikes and demonstrations by construction workers have taken place since that time as well. Workers in these actions protested nonpayment of wages, living conditions at labor camps, and lack of a minimum wage.[13] Unwittingly, the state's segregation of workers into work camps facilitated their efforts to organize, fostering, writes Buckley, a shop floor politics "in which the workplace and the mass-worker household would become integral to the development of the labour movement" (2013, 266). This was met with violent state repression: mass arrests, summary deportation of strikers labeled "instigators," planting plainclothes police informants, beatings, and turning off air conditioning at residential compounds as a form of punishment. But such attempts at coercion only emboldened workers, who mobilized a massive two-week strike of thirty thousand to forty thousand workers in November 2007. By 2008, the Dubai state responded with a less coercive strategy of privatizing labor relations. From then on, labor conflicts were to be directed to the employer rather than to the Ministry of Labour. This both helped avoid the formation of unions and, as Buckley writes, rendered labor protests "both *discreet* and *discrete*: not only was labour unrest largely removed from the view of the media, the public and real estate investors, but privatization also served to separate and divide striking groups from the actions of workers from different companies or projects who might otherwise have had an opportunity to join forces" (2013, 266–269).[14]

What is remarkable about this story of organized labor resistance to exploitation both yielding improved conditions for workers and eventuating in new capitalist strategies of labor discipline is how unremarkable it is. It is echoed by similar such events in the at least two-hundred-year history of industrial capitalism. What is also worth noting is that these events are unexceptional not only in a historical sense but also in a geographic one. While such labor exploitation, particularly in its more violent and coercive forms, has often been discussed as particular to the supposedly "illiberal" South, an increasing literature is pointing out that it is also characteristic of the supposedly "liberal" North (Hannah, Bauder, and Shields 2016; Lewis et al. 2015; R. Vogel 2006, 2007; Wise 2013). Even the social democratic Nordic region so often celebrated by self-styled American social democrats is no exception, as the migration scholar Natalia Ollus (2016) has discussed. In Finland, for example, she points out that the most precarious workers are migrants, particularly women, whose rights are routinely infringed on by employers as a means of increasing exploitation. Employers she interviewed complained of having no choice in hyperexploitation, citing fierce competition in globalized labor markets. One cannot help but note the echoes to Marx's quip about the capitalist's soul as the soul of capital, who regardless of her or his personal qualities must submit to the iron law of capitalist competition (Marx 1976, 342). By contrast, workers who spoke to Ollus expressed the "paradoxical" (Ollus's word) conundrum of being forced into flexibility—that is, of being forced to be "willing" to take any job available, and also fearing losing jobs that they knew to be exploitative. There is, of course, nothing paradoxical in this. It is an acute expression of the alienation arising from the contradictory compelled "freedom" to earn a wage in any capitalist society, what Marx (1976, 899) called the "silent compulsion of economic relations" under capitalism.

Marxist concepts of exploitation, production of surplus value, and social reproduction raise worthwhile questions in relation both to ethnography and to regional study approaches critical of neoliberal paradigms. Critiques of the culture concept have reoriented anthropology and ethnographic sociology toward far greater sensitivity to the ways our case studies are shaped by and can in turn inform analysis of global processes and interconnections (Abu-Lughod 1992; Gupta and Ferguson 1996; Mamdani 2004). Moving away from older notions of culture and cultural relativism and toward seeing our specific field sites as shot through with global dynamics of power, economics, and history has been, as any intellectual advance dialectically is, simultaneously a process of discovery and of anamnesis, of remembering and recognition. As Lila Abu-Lughod (2013) has eloquently written, to move away from "culture" as an analytic category and toward one of "respecting difference" means recognizing that Western and especially US-based ethnographers have always already been interconnected with the supposed "non-West." This is not to promote some sort of feel-good world culture narrative. Abu-Lughod's culture critique is, simultaneously, a political critique, directed squarely at the bloodthirsty American empire. Bringing in the Gulf and de-exceptionalizing it builds on the aforementioned reorientation of ethnographic social science, highlighting the mechanics of exploitation that form much of the substance, and in all cases the condition of possibility, of global interconnection. While respecting differences is necessary, this difference must be understood as shaped by larger global patterns. The concrete reality of the current labor regime in the Gulf, and in particular in rapidly urbanizing places like Doha and Dubai, makes a strong case for de-exceptionalizing the region in the ways we have been discussing in this book.

Conclusion

A Marxist perspective on de-exceptionalization of the Arabian Peninsula is particularly suitable to the topic of this chapter because of the centrality of labor exploitation to it. This explicit Marxist perspective, moreover, complements the one informed by anti-Orientalism and postcolonial critique. The issue of labor exploitation is central because of how prominent the bodies and images of foreign workers have been, especially those from South Asia, to exceptionalizing Western liberal discourses that, drawing on earlier Orientalist repertoires of cultural and geographic representation, have used these workers to construct an image of the region as uniquely exploitative and coercive of low-wage workers. One of the effects of this is to disconnect and distance the Arabian Peninsula from processes of capital and empire arising from the West/North, especially an imperial United States, to whose post–World War II global hegemony the region, particularly the Gulf client states, have been so central. Another result of this binary between Oriental other to the supposedly civilized West is to absolve the latter of regimes of labor exploitation and hyperprecarity that are as characteristic of the contemporary "liberal" North as they are of the "illiberal" South. Finally, such a representational disconnect serves to naturalize capitalism. Defenders of capitalism can simply refer to the kinds of exploitation that occur in places like the Qatar, the UAE, and others, and categorize them as deviant from the supposedly civilized version that prevails in the North/West. As I have argued in this chapter, and as we have collectively argued in this book, such thinking succumbs to the illusion of cultural boundedness and excises the Arabian

Peninsula from global patterns of history, politics, and social process, as well as from Western complicity in regional dynamics of power. As we discuss in the conclusion, our critical project here has been to counteract the related process of exceptionalizing and decentering of the Arabian Peninsula, highlighting why this project is of more than just academic interest.

Notes

1. See Khalaf 1992 on the "image of unlimited good" in the Gulf.

2. By "whiteness," I mean the ways in which elites of Arabian Peninsula, and particularly Gulf, societies have historically privileged white racialized subjects from Europe and North America in areas ranging from spatial segregation and labor market discrimination to representations of national authenticity, in which South Asian and African contributions to Arabian Peninsula societies have been downplayed. See Khalifa 2006.

3. I use the term "worker residence" or "housing compound" because I want to avoid the connections that the term "labor camp" has with the history of European racism and colonialism. For early and pioneering contributions to the demystification of Gulf workers' experiences, see Gamburd 2000 and Khalaf and Alkobaisi 1999. Ahmad 2017 and Gardner 2010 are later and valuable contributions.

4. By "absolute surplus value," I mean the kind of surplus value that is yielded by the extension of labor time or the intensification of the exploitation of the laborer. It is the subject of a long and important section of volume 1 of *Capital* (Marx 1976, 281–426).

5. Even in the North, the idea of a specifically neoliberal hyperprecarity marginalizes forms of hyperprecarity that preceded the usual historiography of neoliberalism, such as racialized and gendered labor that arguably never or at most very briefly benefited from Keynesian and social democratic state interventions (Federici 2004).

6. During my fieldwork in the early 2000s, one of the local features of urban life celebrated in local news coverage of international meetings such as that of the World Trade Organization that converged on cities like Doha and Dubai was the lack of protests or urban unrest surrounding such meetings. This was in contrast to the massive protests in cities such as Seattle in 1999 and Genoa in 2001.

7. Emphasis in original.

8. It is important to note that not all Gulf nationals have benefited from this spatial fix, as it has helped produce new and more efficient forms of state control and has furthered projects of accumulation by dispossession (Menoret 2014). This has especially impacted historically marginalized groups such as the bedouins and bidoon. Relatedly, a large number of, in particular, Saudi and Bahraini nationals, and a not insignificant minority in the other Gulf countries, are employed in low-wage jobs, including taxi drivers, cashiers, government employment, and agricultural employment.

9. Attiya Ahmad's (2017) detailed and theoretically astute work on the ways that women workers in Kuwait exercise agency over their lives, and in particular in forming networks of support through religious conversion, is a must-read.

10. See migrant-rights.org, "Domestic Workers in the Gulf," 2019, https://www .migrant-rights.org/statistic/domesticworkers/.

11. Human Rights Watch, "I Already Bought You: Abuse and Exploitation of Female Migrant Domestic Workers in the United Arab Emirate," October 22, 2014, https:// www.hrw.org/report/2014/10/22/i-already-bought-you/abuse-and-exploitation-female -migrant-domestic-workers-united.

12. Human Rights Watch, "I Already Bought You."

13. The year 2007, in particular, seems to have been especially marked by labor un- rest (Buckley 2013, 265–66).

14. As Nancy MacLean (2017) brilliantly shows, outlawing industry-wide worker organization, or enshrining into law the "right" of workers to negotiate only with their own boss, has been a key element of the neoliberal project for decades. It was one of the main features of Augusto Pinochet's so-called Constitution of Liberty of 1980, drafted in collaboration with American neoliberal economists, as well as of antilabor politics in the United States since the founding of the Mont Pelerin Society in 1947.

CONCLUSION

Centering the Arabian Peninsula, Decolonizing the Academy

AHMED KANNA, AMÉLIE LE RENARD, NEHA VORA

This book began as a series of informal conversations among us about how inherited knowledges and mappings of the Arabian Peninsula as both exceptional and disconnected from other parts of the world shaped our early approaches to fieldwork and ethnographic writing. Soon the conversations expanded into the role played by academic, journalistic, and other received knowledge in the shaping of ethnography in general, and how the Gulf might be particularly well situated to shed light on the interplay among "common sense," field research, and anthropological writing. We took important insights from feminist, Marxist, and postcolonial theory that the social scientist's perspective and social scientific knowledge are always shaped by their ideological and spatiotemporal situatedness to ask in what ways exceptionalist representations of the region have operated with the illusion of objectivity. We were interested in the politics that have shaped the conditions by which the Gulf and the Arabian Peninsula have been produced as an object of study, the role of colonial and imperial histories, gendered and racial logics, and contemporary geopolitics. At the most general level, this volume can be read as an attempt to both replace ideas of cultural essence with those of social process and assert that ethnographic fieldwork is, in itself, a social process that reveals much about the societies we study, provided we as ethnographers question our own embodied experience in the process.

As we wrote in the introduction, attending closely to social process at the very beginning of any research should not be read as constituting a "critical" perspective, as it is often taken to be, but should be the normative entry point for any inquiry into study of the Arabian Peninsula. Orientalist ideas about the region, its internal coherence, and its inhabitants unfortunately are still deeply held and often prop up state narratives about who can claim rightful national belonging, what forms of rule are natural, and which histories are legitimate. This is more than an academic point. At the time of writing, Europe and the United States are experiencing a right-wing backlash against immigrants, poor people, and all in vulnerable and nonnormative subject positions. Meanwhile, Middle Eastern regimes from Saudi Arabia to Israel to Syria justify their military campaigns, devastating impoverished, spatially incarcerated populations from Palestine to Yemen, by themselves positioning their political opponents as terrorists, uncivilized, or foreign. Recourse to essentialized understandings of Islamic tradition and Arab cultural essence are also used to prop up patriarchal and homophobic repression, erasing complex histories of gender and sexuality fluidity and women's political and economic power, as well as limiting the access of marginalized groups to education, health care, political representation, and other rights and resources.

In this book, we have looked at how both Western interventions and local elites have drawn on and deployed logics of cultural essence and Orientalist ideas, but we have also attempted to go beyond this. Complementing the discursive critique of Orientalism, we examined the contours of Arabian Peninsula exceptionalism to highlight not only representational practices but also the role of global political economy, of transnational cultural interconnection, and of histories of imperialism and capitalism, both in contemporary local societies and in constituting the field in which and about which ethnographers research and write. These interconnections and global histories, and the ways they have impacted daily life in the Arabian Peninsula, the ways that they shape the production and reproduction of societies in the region, have been generally de-emphasized in knowledge production until recently. Instead, the region has been seen as an exception to transnational processes of capitalism, empire, social contradiction, and class struggle for much too long. In addition to highlighting the ordinary and interconnected aspects of everyday life through the ethnographic chapters in this book, we also wanted to explore how deeply impactful Western imaginative geographies are on researchers, including ourselves, and thus we spent one chapter discussing the baggage we unconsciously carried with us as we began our work. The centrality of reflexivity in our work is due both to the very different experiences we each had based on our gendered, raced, and linguistic positions in our field sites, and to the expectations we brought with us, and hopefully highlights to other readers why reflexivity is so important to bring not only to fieldwork and ethnographic writing in/on the Arabian Peninsula but to all scholarship. Exceptionalizing frameworks, as we hope we have begun to illuminate here, impact every aspect of knowledge production for ethnographers and their interlocutors, and even the built environment itself, and our experiences of it.

As our conversations developed around the different chapters, reflexivity about academia itself and the power relations that construct hierarchies between universities, scholars, journals, books, and forms of knowledge emerged as central in our exchanges. Here, we argue that de-exceptionalizing the Arabian Peninsula as a field site also requires deconstructing an idealized vision of Western academia as a presumed site of democracy and liberalism. The projects of anthropology and sociology, as they have been invested in anticolonial and antiracist justice and breaking down binary understandings between East and West, self and other, civilized and savage, are implicated in the continuing use of the exceptional and spectacular as tropes in ethnographic writing, revealing just how much work is yet to be done within our disciplines. Within these disciplines, some have questioned the various hierarchies that are realized through the production of knowledge, not only between the social scientists and their "objects" or "fields," but also among social scientists themselves, particularly the ways in which power relations in terms of status, racialized identification, class, and gender shape perceptions of their expertise or lack thereof. But these questionings tend to be too marginalized to transform actual practices. In 2018, reports of abuses of power at the journal HAU, the self-described journal of ethnographic theory, led to significant discussion among academics online, particularly BIPOC (Black Indigenous People of Color), women, graduate students, and junior faculty, that inspired us to develop some of the broader questions we bring forward below about the possible impacts of this volume beyond scholarship on the region.

Centering the Arabian Peninsula

While this book has focused on the GCC states, but particularly the UAE, Qatar, and Saudi Arabia through case studies of Dubai, Doha, and Riyadh, we are interested not in reifying an imagined idea of a homogenous cultural and social landscape of the Arabian Peninsula but rather in challenging the way that "Gulf Studies" as a project has created a narrow focus on the region that privileges top-down state-centric approaches at the expense of interdisciplinary, ethnographic, locally grounded, historical, and transnational analyses. The categories that scholars, journalists, and pundits have naturalized to understand and explain the people, places, temporalities, and politics of the Arabian Peninsula are based in geopolitical and academic genealogies of empire: first British and now also American. As ethnographers, we have had to struggle against these naturalizations in formulating our research questions, in navigating our field sites, in representing our interlocutors, and in gaining legitimacy for our work among our peers within area studies and beyond. But denaturalizing both region and the categories that are ascribed to the region has allowed us to ask questions about what knowledge that starts in the field site might look like, with knowledge producers outside of the Global North, and ask about connections between what are considered emic or exceptional phenomena and other parts of the world.

One of the images particularly salient in our minds as we developed our thoughts along these lines was of the Gulf as supposedly exceptional owing to its oil resources. Oil is often cited as the source of the region's so-called pathologies, as well as its wealth. The *tafra naftiyya*, or "oil leap," was both an emic category deployed by our Gulf Arab interlocutors, especially among managerial professional strata, and the key to all the supposed riddles presented by Gulf societies, when seen from outside. Petrodollars piled up in Gulf state treasuries and were recycled as handouts to citizens, who became grateful, silent, and lazy. But, then, if Gulf societies are pathological oil societies, what does that make Western ones, the United States above all? For isn't the infamous "American dream" itself an oil-based ideology? What other material condition made possible the single-family-occupancy houses, interstate highways, suburbs, and shopping malls through which the postwar American white heteronormative "good life" could be realized? (Huber 2013). Indeed, what other material condition makes possible the American and neoliberal concept of democracy as an elite, top-down planning practice managed and distributed by a few wealthy capitalists, to the exclusion of other, more expansive definitions of democracy? (Mitchell 2011). And what part of the world, other than the Arabian Peninsula itself, has been as indispensable in providing the petrodollars and military bases necessary to prop up the postwar American finance capital dominated order? (Hanieh 2011). Another parallel to draw is the use of so-called counterterrorist measures to repress any critique of the government, a widespread process we can observe in many contemporary states. In Saudi Arabia in the 2000s, many people suspected to be close to "jihadi Islamist" dissent were imprisoned without trial; in the 2010s, the ban on public protest was reasserted, and many political opponents with various orientations were accused of "terrorism," dozens of them sentenced to death. Though the modalities and scale of violence depend on context, the use of counterterrorism to repress opponents is far from exceptional, blurring, once again, the liberal/illiberal dichotomy. In France in the aftermath of the 2015 shootings, the state of emergency was adopted and many protest marches were banned; counterterrorist measures targeted people that were supposedly close to "radical Islam" but also leftists, through searches and house arrests. Since then, social movements have been increasingly criminalized, as many experienced through the violent repression of protest marches in 2018–2019 (more than 2,000 wounded). The governmental production of counterterrorist consent and how it has been used to repress criticism would be interesting to compare in different political contexts.

Another supposed exception characterizing the Arabian Peninsula that we have challenged is the practice of kafala. The management of migrants often interpreted as exceptional under the term "kafala" can be put in perspective with what is happening in the United States and fortress Europe, for example. Migration under contemporary global capitalism to many European and North American countries is precarious and exploitative. The states of the wealthy North premise their migration regimes, to put it mildly, not on principles of the universal right to movement or human rights but on temporary labor needs and militarized borders. Anti-immigration policies, including the various measures meant to prevent migrants from asking for asylum, engender hundreds of deaths every year in the Mediterranean Sea and at various borders and roads to European countries; these policies also result in similar kinds of harm and human rights violations, from family separations to sexual assault to death, on the US-Mexico border. While kafala makes domestic workers extremely dependent from their employers, such dependence also exists, with different modalities, in many regimes of labor migration, without even mentioning marriage migration, an instituted and normalized dependence. Gendered exploitation of both male and female migrant workers in the Arabian Peninsula is also paradigmatic of global capitalism, as Ahmed explored in chapter 4 (see also Ahmad 2017; Mahdavi 2016; Parrenas 2000). It is far from specific to the region, as seen, for instance, in the case of seasonal female Moroccan workers in Spain, employed on very short-term contracts in agriculture, in the framework of a binational program aimed to provide a workforce while preventing more permanent immigration to the EU: the employers choose poor divorced or widowed women with young kids in order to make sure they go back to Morocco at the end of the season, exploiting their precarity and family situations (Arab 2018). On the other hand, we have unpacked how the charges of "modern day slavery" levied on Gulf labor regimes both elide the violence of chattel slavery and diminish the ways that poor workers are exploited in other parts of the world (Vora 2013b; Vora and Koch 2015). The privileges of white/Western residents and the essentialization of whiteness/Westernness as expertise reveal the current global racialized hierarchies between universities, diplomas, and people. The ways in which nation, class, and race are articulated in global cities of the Arabian Peninsula may help us de-essentialize Westernness and look at how privileges of mobility and class are often tied to one's passport nationality (see also Ong 1999). Seen in this context, the hierarchies of "ethnocracy" that are often ascribed to the Gulf are not exceptional but rather part of regional and even international orderings of belonging and human value.

While gender and sexuality issues in the Peninsula are common objects of exceptionalization through the trope of the oppressed Muslim woman or rampant homophobia attributed to so-called Wahhabi Islam, some processes analyzed in the Peninsula may also help us understand global transformations. The policing of public spaces in contexts such as Dubai and Riyadh is part of a widening vision of gendered and racialized security and surveillance, as the penalization of street harassment seen increasingly in more states shows. It tends to construct public spaces as dangerous for women, seen as victims, and to racialize male foreign workers as threatening, while ignoring the many abuses against women in private houses—abuses that spouses, partners, relatives, or employers of domestic workers commit—as well as the precarity of subalternized men in public spaces. On the other hand, the ways that gender-segregated spaces may enable a wide range of femininities and masculinities, including queer and trans subjectivities, are most often rendered invisible, since homonationalism, as a hegemonic discursive formation, represents the West as a safe haven for LGBT people, despite hegemonic heteronormativity and various conservative attacks against their rights, especially by Christian fundamentalists (Puar 2007). In this regard, it would be interesting to study the regional and transnational circulations of progressive as well as homophobic and transphobic discourses, with their diverse references to religion, psychology, and geopolitics. What would it mean to center the Arabian Peninsula in research questions about larger contemporary processes such as these?

As ethnographers of the Arabian Peninsula, we are relatively peripheralized in our academic fields. Study of the region is far from central in US anthropology, for example. Ahmed, one of the US-based authors, remembers that even anthropologists who were pathbreakers in the critical turn of the 1980s and 1990s dismissed the Gulf as a field site when he first began his work there, unconsciously repeating the well-known stereotype we critique in this book: that the Gulf is not where "authentic" Arab culture exists. Similarly, Neha was told by Middle East studies faculty that Dubai was a place without "culture." This marginalization of the region was reflected more generally in the almost total lack of ethnographic and social scientific knowledge produced on the Arabian Peninsula, beyond the trope of "coffee pots and camels" that Paul Dresch (2000) has noted. Ironically, as we have discussed in this book, the region has mostly been reduced to nothing but culture. These stereotyped representations were also applied to Yemen, a country directly allied with the United States, which allowed access to researchers in the US academy, a situation that, as we show in this book, began to change over the past two decades. In France too, the Arabian Peninsula is peripheralized; scholarship on the region is considered as specific, while works on France are supposedly general. In the (transnational) field of Gulf studies, researchers focusing on subjects that governments construct as strategic, especially those related to Islamic militancy and oil, get specific resources, from think tank grants to book prizes. In relation to Saudi Arabia, such subjects were hegemonic when Amélie began her research in the 2000s. Only a final panel in conferences was usually devoted to "society," and this is where she would present her paper in gender studies. While the researchers, who were predominantly white males, were curious to know about Saudi women they did not have access to, some asked what the "big" political issues at stake were with such a "small" subject.

Hierarchy among subjects of study, which often articulates with other social hierarchies, impacts publications, careers, and access to resources. The image of some subjects as "serious" facilitates publishing in major area studies journals and with career recruitment. How might centering not only the Arabian Peninsula but gender, sexuality, race, household, and other topics that have until now been seen as marginal provide us with better information about the societies we study as well as transnational processes, globalization, and the contemporary world?

Reflecting on the Academy

In June 2018, as we were working on this manuscript, former and current staff members at the journal HAU published two anonymous open letters detailing a range of allegations against the journal's editor in chief, Giovanni da Col (who was ultimately suspended from his position).[1] The allegations included misogyny and sexual harassment, workplace abuse, failure to pay wages on time, financial misconduct such as misuse of journal funds and overcharging authors and institutions, and making unilateral decisions about the journal's direction without consulting the editorial board, which resulted in an erosion of its open access mission. Following the publication of these letters, several anthropologists and others associated with da Col, with HAU, or with the core group of scholars and institutions involved with the journal's success started writing about their own experiences, mostly corroborating that the culture at this journal had been toxic for quite some time. Others came to the defense of HAU and argued that this was just one "bad apple," that HAU was a pioneering journal that published cutting-edge anthropology, and that its open access format was democratizing an otherwise elitist project: academic publishing. Like many fields, anthropology was experiencing a Me Too movement, but one that centered not only gendered violence but its imbrication in colonized knowledge practices and institutions. The hashtags #hautalk and #AnthroTwitter (and later #refuseHAU) quickly erupted over the next few weeks as scholars began discussing the larger dynamics within anthropology that the responses to HAU brought to light. Twitter allowed anthropologists from a range of backgrounds to weigh in on how a culture of complicity is not unique to HAU but rather quite normal within anthropology, especially at top-tier institutions, and within North American and European academia more broadly. #Hautalk opened up space for conversations about ongoing colonization, patriarchy, elitism, and white supremacy in anthropology and the academy. This echoed movements in other contexts contesting widespread abuse—for instance, through the denunciation of harassers in Indian universities, or criticizing the coloniality of academia, such as the "Rhodes must fall" movement in South Africa.[2] Because these conversations took place primarily on Twitter and other online platforms, contingent faculty, graduate students, indigenous scholars, Global South anthropologists, and others who are not usually centered with the discipline were able to lead much of the discussion. For example, there has been a great deal of discussion about how citational economies reproduce existing hierarchies even as they claim to take stances that are feminist, antiracist, Marxist, or decolonial.[3]

The "Writing Culture" moment clearly showed us that citation needs to be part of any revolution in the academy: a white-male-led attention to representational politics only resulted in a discipline that remained white public space. Furthermore, anthropology cannot be decolonized if we continue to perpetuate an understanding of the world in which theory's location stands in opposition to that of the people it studies.[4] The naming of HAU itself, taken from a Maori word, highlighted how twenty-first-century anthropology continues to feel perfectly comfortable appropriating indigenous knowledge but not including indigenous people as scholarly colleagues on editorial boards or in other prestigious positions.[5] HAU and its defenders—the apology letters, claims of a few "bad apples," posts that begged scholars not to stop citing the "good" works that were published by the journal, and in some cases vitriolic backlash against already precarious scholars by senior established faculty—were a symptom of the myths of liberalism and the liberal academy (see also Mahmud 2016; Vora 2018). This myth believes that the academy is inherently good (and separated from state, military, and capitalist interests), that it will self-correct when it goes astray, and that it is on a path of perpetual progress. This liberal mythology also underpins anthropology and underwrites the inequalities that shape the discipline. It also hinders a truly decolonial and egalitarian discipline and academy, because it is liberalism itself that justified the very things it claims to disavow: colonialism, racism, misogyny, and class.

This liberal mythology is foundational to exceptionalist discourses on the Arabian Peninsula. Our research showed us that exceptionalism among white/Western residents and researchers often presupposes an idealized vision of Western societies as democratic, egalitarian, and/or liberal (see also Koch 2017). Reflecting on our places in Gulf cities and reasserting these cities' role in global networks encouraged us to consider academics in the wider framework of global power relations. We were trained, as academics, to conceive of ourselves as outsiders not influencing the societies that we are studying. However, the global power relations that make Western/white professional expertise highly valued in the region, as we have explored in this book, also make knowledge on the region produced in Western universities more valued globally than any other knowledge about the region. Works in women's and gender studies produced in Saudi universities, for instance, are rarely published as accessible books, and many are unreferenced on the Internet. Language is an issue, but it is not the only one.

The current lack of visibility for works produced in the Arabian Peninsula results from various processes that relate to postcoloniality. On the one hand, the most visible research on the Arabian Peninsula is published in English-language books targeted at Anglophone readers, and selected following specific, exclusive criteria of excellence (which often include affiliation with elite Western institutions). Many of them never get translated and/or distributed in the Arabian Peninsula (except for their circulation in elite branch campuses, which are connected to the imperial processes we are discussing here). The global hegemony of US and British norms of academic writing and the asymmetry they produce in terms of what analysis gets published, read, and quoted pertain to the coloniality of knowledge (Mignolo 2002; Quijano 2000). Our research, through funding, access, and publishing, is entangled in global power relations that make it both more visible and recognized than research conducted in most universities of the Arabian Peninsula (and Ahmed and Neha in particular as US-based academics who publish in English). We argue that research on the Arabian Peninsula needs to include reflexivity on imperialism, geopolitics, and racial capitalism, in the field and in broader social science.

On the other hand, the regimes supported by the United States and the United Kingdom in the Arabian Peninsula had until recently rather discouraged, if not repressed, the local production and publishing of critical social science, except for expertise-oriented approaches and statistics. However, other forms of writing and of knowledge, which are less valued in academic circles, circulate. Abdul Rahman Munif's *Cities of Salt* (published in Arabic between 1984 and 1989) may be the most famous narrative of imperialism in the Peninsula (Munif 1987, 1991, 1993). Novelists have dealt with subjects that are relatively absent in fieldwork-based research, such as the first wave of Palestinian migration experiences to Kuwait in Ghassan Kanafani's *Men in the Sun* (1999 [1962]), the exploitation faced by Malayali rural workers in *Goat Days* by Benyamin (2012 [2008]), Arab women's migration to Najd as spouses and teachers in *Al-Bahriyat* by Umayma Al-Khamis (2006), or the life of inhabitants with African descent in the Hejaz, in *Maymûna* by Mahmûd Trawrî (2007). The vibrant artist and activist communities in cities such as Dubai, Kuwait City, Doha, and Abu Dhabi highlight an interest in learning about each other across supposedly hardened class and ethnonational lines, as do the online spaces that link into these communities, which also allow greater access for those who cannot easily exist in public spaces due to gender, sexuality, race, or class. Some examples of these projects (which number in the dozens, if not more) include Madeenah, a collective that provides walking tours of Kuwait's architecture;[6] Doha Fashion Fridays, which highlights the personalities and fashion of migrant workers;[7] the Ensaniyat project, which aims to educate Kuwait's residents about workers' rights through art projects;[8] and the programing put on by gallery spaces such as Third Eye and Al Serkal Avenue in Dubai's Al Quoz district. De-exceptionalizing the field may encourage us to take into account these productions as valuable accounts of Arabian Peninsula societies' complex histories and dynamics, especially as researchers, with few exceptions such as the work of anthropologist Elizabeth Derderian on UAE artists (Derderian 2019), have ignored important issues tackled by artists and writers in the Peninsula, aside from the exceptionalist representation of the "taboo." More generally, it should motivate us to reexamine the authors we quote and the objects we construct, and to center race, migration, class, gender, and sexuality in our research. The confluence of war in other parts of the Middle East, as well as in Yemen, and funding channeled to higher-education institutions in the Arabian Peninsula (both of which are connected to the region's entanglement with geopolitics of empire and capital, as we have discussed throughout the book) has made Gulf studies more prominent within Middle East studies and our disciplines of anthropology and sociology in the past decade. Scholars are finding more conferences, funding opportunities, programs of study, and teaching positions in/on the region, and these are all becoming more internationally recognized. The growth of new campuses, many of which are affiliated with Western universities, has made Gulf cities into emerging academic hubs in the region, as part of state strategies for knowledge economy development and post-oil economic diversification. The extent to which these campuses are achieving those goals has yet to be seen, but there is a large amount of contestation, from both residents and those outside the Gulf—many who are based at "home" campuses of the universities expanding into the region—about what it means to bring Western and liberal forms of education into supposedly illiberal spaces. While these kinds of skepticism rightfully question the motivations behind large-scale spending and who mega-development projects might be benefiting, they continue to propagate the liberal myths that we have been describing as central to both the project of the academy and regional exceptionalism. These campuses, as those who have been researching them on the ground have begun to explore (like Neha in her work on Doha's Education City [see chapter 3 and Vora 2014b, 2015, 2018]), with their hybrid norms of teaching and mixed classes, may become viable sites of alternate knowledge production. New PhD programs at the Qatar Faculty of Islamic Studies, the Doha Institute, and Qatar University's Gulf Studies Center, for example, are drawing students from the Global South who are interested in ethnographically exploring forms of religiosity, identity, culture, and social networks among various resident communities in Qatar. This kind of fieldwork is novel to regional studies and can challenge existing narratives of "Wahhabism," Sunni/Shi'i "sectarianism," Islamic conversion, and the idea that Muslim immigrants are outsiders who do not interact with Qataris or influence Arabian forms of religion. We hope that South-South research that decenters "the West" will keep growing in places like these, further transforming the categories we have both to theorize the region and to form the basis of a truly internationalist ethnography, which can serve as a resource to better understand how transnational and global phenomena shape daily life in other parts of the world.

Notes

1. "An Open Letter from the Former HAU Staff 7," Footnotes, June 13, 2018, https://footnotesblog.com/2018/06/13/guest-post-an-open-letter-from-the-former-hau-staff-7/; "Former and Current HAU Staff Letter," June 14, 2018, https://haustaffletter.wordpress.com/; "Statement of HAU Board of Trustees," June 29, 2018, https://www.haujournal.org/index.php/hau/announcement/view/21.

2. Nayanika Mathur, "Shocked, Not Surprised," Allegra Lab, June 22, 2018, http://allegralaboratory.net/shocked-not-surprised-hautalk/.

3. Jules Weiss, "Citation Is a Gift: 'Punking Accounting' in #hautalk," Footnotes, July 7, 2018, https://footnotesblog.com/2018/07/07/guest-post-citation-is-a-gift-punking-accounting-in-hautalk/.

4. See also Zoe Todd, "The Decolonial Turn 2.0: The Reckoning," June 15, 2018, https://anthrodendum.org/2018/06/15/the-decolonial-turn-2-0-the-reckoning/.

5. Mahi Tahi Collective, "An Open Letter to the HAU Journal's Board of Trustees," Association of Social Anthropologists of Aotearoa/New Zealand, June 18, 2018, http://www.asaanz.org/blog/2018/6/18/an-open-letter-to-the-hau-journals-board-of-trustees.

6. See the Instagram page for Madeenah, which describes itself as follows: "Madeenah is a multidisciplinary platform that curates cultural tours and delivers spatial studies," accessed October 25, 2019, https://www.instagram.com/madeenahkw/.

7. See the Instagram page for Doha Fashion Fridays, accessed October 25, 2019, https://www.instagram.com/dohafashionfridays/?hl=en.

8. Ensaniyat Project, which describes itself as "A project aimed at spreading knowledge and awareness about Migrant/Domestic Workers Rights and Laws in Kuwait and Qatar," accessed October 25, 2019, https://www.instagram.com/ensaniyatproject/?utm_source=ig_embed.

Bibliography

Abu-Lughod, Lila. 1991. "Writing against Culture." In *Recapturing Anthropology: Working in the Present*, edited by R. G. Fox, 137–62. Santa Fe, NM: School of American Research Press.

——, ed. 1998. *Remaking Women: Feminism and Modernity in the Middle East*. Princeton, NJ: Princeton University Press.

——. 2001. "*Orientalism* and Middle East Feminist Studies." *Feminist Studies* 27 (1): 101–13.

——. 2013. *Do Muslim Women Need Saving?* Cambridge, MA: Harvard University Press.

Adelkhah, Fariba. 2001. "Dubaï: Capitale Économique de l'Iran?" In *Dubaï*, edited by Roland Marchal, 39–65. Paris: CNRS Editions.

Ahmad, Attiya. 2011. "Beyond Labor: Foreign Residents in the Gulf States." In *Migrant Labor in the Gulf*, edited by Mehran Kamrava and Zahra Babar, 21–40. Doha: Center for International and Regional Studies, Georgetown School of Foreign Service Qatar.

——. 2017. *Everyday Conversions: Islam, Domestic Work, and South Asian Migrant Women in Kuwait*. Durham, NC: Duke University Press.

Ahmadi, Ameena. 2015. "A City for Education." *Architectural Design: Special Issue: UAE and The Gulf: Architecture and Urbanism* 85(1): 46–53.

Ahmed, Leila. 1992. *Women and Gender in Islam: Historical Roots of a Modern Debate*. New Haven, CT: Yale University Press.

Ahmed, Sara. 2000. *Strange Encounters. Embodied Others in Post-Coloniality*. London: Routledge.

Aksan, Virginia. 2010. "How Do We 'Know' the Middle East?" *Review of Middle East Studies* 44 (1): 3–12.

Al Kuwari, Ali Khalifa. 2012. "The People Want Reform . . . in Qatar, Too." Jadaliyya. December 10, 2012. http://www.jadaliyya.com/pages/index/8880/the.

Al Sayegh, Fatma. 1998. "Merchants' Role in a Changing Society: The Case of Dubai, 1900–90." *Middle Eastern Studies* 34 (1): 87–102.

Al Shehabi, Omar, Adam Hanieh, and Abdulhadi Khalaf, eds. 2014. *Transit States: Labour, Migration and Citizenship in the Gulf.* London: Pluto Press.

Ali, Syed. 2010. *Dubai: Gilded Cage.* New Haven, CT: Yale University Press.

Al-Khamis, Umayma. 2006. *Al-Bahriyat.* Damascus: Al-Mada.

Al-Khatîb, Salwâ. 2008. *Muqaddima fî 'ilm al-anthrûbûlûjiyyâ.* Al-Qâhira; Al-Riyâdh: al-tibâ'a al-misriyya li-khadmât al-tibâ'a.

Alloula, Malek. 1981. *Le harem colonial: Images d'un sous-érotisme.* Paris: Slatkine.

Almana, Aisha. 1981. "Economic Development and Its Impact on the Status of Woman in Saudi Arabia." PhD thesis, University of Colorado Boulder.

Al-Mughni, Haya. 2001. *Women in Kuwait: The Politics of Gender.* London: Saqi Books.

Al-Nakib, Farah. 2016. *Kuwait Transformed: A History of Oil and Urban Life.* Palo Alto, CA: Stanford University Press.

Al-Qasimi, Noor. 2011. "Ladies and Gentlemen, Boyahs and Girls: Uploading Transnational Queer Subjectivities in the United Arab Emirates." In *Circuits of Visibility: Gender and Transnational Media Culture*, edited by Radha Hedge, 284–302. New York: NYU Press.

Al-Rasheed, Madawi. 2013. *A Most Masculine State: Gender, Politics, and Religion in Saudi Arabia.* Cambridge, MA: Cambridge University Press.

——. 2016. *Muted Modernists: The Struggle over Divine Politics in Saudi Arabia.* New York: Oxford University Press.

Al-Rasheed, Madawi, and Robert Vitalis. 2004. *Counter-Narratives: History, Contemporary Society, and Politics in Saudi Arabia and Yemen.* New York: Palgrave Macmillan.

Arebi, Saddeka. 1994. *Women and Words in Saudi Arabia. The Politics of Literary Discourse.* New York: Columbia University Press.

Altorki, Soraya, and Donald Cole. 1989. *Arabian Oasis City: The Transformation of 'Unaiza.* Austin: University of Texas Press.

Arab, Chadia. 2018. *Dames de fraises, doigts de fée, les invisibles de la migration marocaine saisonnière en Espagne.* Casablanca: En Toutes Lettres.

Asad, Talal, ed. 1973. *Anthropology and the Colonial Encounter.* Ithaca, NY: Ithaca Press.

——. 1993. *Genealogies of Religion.* Baltimore: Johns Hopkins University Press.

Assaf, Laure. 2017. "Jeunesses arabes d'Abou Dhabi (Émirats arabes unis): Catégories statutaires, sociabilités urbaines et modes de subjectivation." PhD diss., Université Paris Ouest Nanterre La Défense.

Bacchetta, Paola. 2015. "Décoloniser le féminisme: Intersectionnalité, assemblages, co-formations, co-productions." *Les cahiers du CEDREF* 20. http://cedref.revues.org/833.

Badger, Sam, Giorgio Cafiero, and Foreign Policy in Focus. 2014. "Kingdom of Slaves in the Gulf." *The Nation*, September 16, 2014. https://www.thenation.com/article/kingdom-slaves-persian-gulf/.

Barrow, Clyde W. 1990. *Universities and the Capitalist State*. Madison: University of Wisconsin Press.

Beaugrand, Claire. 2017. *Stateless in the Gulf: Migration, Nationality and Society in Kuwait*. London: IB Tauris.

Benhabib, Seyla. 2011. "Why I Oppose Yale in Singapore." *Yale News*, May 18, 2011. http://yaledailynews.com/blog/2011/05/18/benhabib-why-i-oppose-yale-in-singapore/.

Benjamin, Walter. 2002. *The Arcades Project*. Edited by H. Eiland. Cambridge, MA: Harvard University Press.

Benyamin, Joseph Koyipally. (2008) 2012. *Goat Days*. New York: Penguin Books. Translated from Malayalam.

Benston, Margaret. 2019 [1969]. "The Political Economy of Women's Liberation." *Monthly Review* 71(4): 1–10.

Bhattacharya, Tithi. 2015. "How Not to Skip Class: Social Reproduction of Labor and the Global Working Class." *Viewpoint Magazine*, October 31, 2015. https://www.viewpointmag.com/2015/10/31/how-not-to-skip-class-social-reproduction-of-labor-and-the-global-working-class/.

Bishara, Fahad Ahmad. 2017. *A Sea of Debt: Law and Economic Life in the Western Indian Ocean, 1780–1950*. New York: Cambridge University Press.

Bogaert, Koen. 2018. *Globalized Authoritarianism: Megaprojects, Slums and Class Relations in Urban Morocco*. Minneapolis: University of Minnesota Press.

Bonnefoy, Laurent. 2018. *Yemen and the World. Beyond Insecurity*. New York: Oxford University Press.

Bonnefoy, Laurent, and Laurence Louër. 2015. "Introduction: The Arab Spring in the Arabian Peninsula and Its aftermath." *Arabian Humanities* 4. http://journals.openedition.org/cy/2896.

Bonnett, Alastair. 2004. *The Idea of the West: Culture, Politics, and History*. New York: Palgrave Macmillan.

Brenner, Johanna. 2017. "Materialism and Feminism." Salvage Quarterly. March 29, 2017. http://salvage.zone/online-exclusive/materialism-and-feminism-an-interview-with-johanna-brenner/.

Breteau, Marion. 2019. "Amours à Mascate. Espaces, rôles de genre et représentations intimes chez les jeunes (sultanat d'Oman)." PhD diss., Université d'Aix-Marseille.

Bristol-Rhys, Jane. 2010. *Emirati Women: Generations of Change*. New York: Oxford University Press.

Bristol-Rhys, Jane, and Caroline Osella. 2016. "Neutralized Bachelors, Infantilized Arabs: Between Migrant and Host Gendered and Sexual Stereotypes in Abu Dhabi." In *Masculinities under Neoliberalism*, edited by A. Cornwall, 111–24. London: Zed Books.

Brodkin, Karen, Sandra Morgan, and Janis Hutchinson. 2011. "Anthropology as White Public Space?" *American Anthropologist* 113 (4): 545–556.

Brown, Jenny. 2019. *Birth Strike: The Hidden Fight over Women's Work*. Oakland, CA: PM Press.

Bsheer, Rosie. 2017. "W(h)ither Arabian Peninsula Studies?" In *The Oxford Handbook of Contemporary Middle-Eastern and North African History*, edited by Jens Hansen and Amal Ghazal. Oxford: Oxford University Press.

———. 2018. "How Mohammed bin Salman Has Transformed Saudi Arabia." Jadaliyya. June 27, 2018. http://www.jadaliyya.com/Details/37696/How-Mohammed-bin-Salman -Has-Transformed-Saudi-Arabia.

Buckley, Michelle. 2013. "Locating Neoliberalism in Dubai: Migrant Workers and Class Struggle in the Autocratic City." *Antipode* 45 (2): 256–274.

———. 2015. "Construction Work, 'Bachelor' Builders and the Intersectional Politics of Urbanization in Dubai." In *Transit States: Labour, Migration and Citizenship in the Gulf*, edited by Omar Al Shehabi, Adam Hanieh, and Abdulhadi Khalaf, 132–152. New York: Pluto Press.

Carapico, Sheila. 2004. "Arabia Incognita: An Invitation to Arabian Peninsula Studies." In *Counter-Narratives: History, Contemporary Society, and Politics in Saudi Arabia and Yemen*, edited by Madawi Al-Rasheed and Robert Vitalis, 11–34. New York: Palgrave Macmillan.

———. 2016. *Arabia Incognita: Dispatches from Yemen and the Gulf*. Charlottesville, VA: Just World Books.

Chalcraft, John. 2011. "Migration and Popular Protest in the Arabian Peninsula and the Gulf in the 1950s and 1960s." *International Labor and Working Class History* 79: 28–47.

Chatterjee, Partha. 1993. *The Nation and Its Fragments: Colonial and Postcolonial Histories*. Princeton, NJ: Princeton University Press.

Chatterjee, Piya, and Sunaina Maira, eds. 2014. *The Imperial University*. Minneapolis: University of Minnesota Press.

Chibber, Vivek. 2013. *Postcolonial Theory and the Specter of Capital*. New York: Verso.

Clancy-Smith, Julia. 2006. "Islam, genre et identités dans la fabrication de l'Algérie française, 1830–1962." *Nouvelles Questions Féministes* 25 (1): 25–40.

Coles, A., and K. Walsh. 2010. "From 'Trucial State' to 'Postcolonial' City? The Imaginative Geographies of British Expatriates in Dubai." *Journal of Ethnic and Migration Studies* 36: 1317–1333.

Coles, Anne, and Anne-Meike Fechter, eds. 2012. *Gender and Family among Transnational Professionals*. New York: Routledge.

Connell, R. W. 1995. *Masculinities*. Berkeley: University of California Press.

Cordesman, Anthony H. 2017. "Saudi Arabia, the UAE, Qatar and the New Game of Thrones." Center for Strategic and International Studies. July 13, 2017. https://www .csis.org/analysis/saudi-arabia-uae-qatar-and-new-game-thrones.

Cosquer, Claire. 2018. "Faire nation hors les murs: Dynamiques migratoires, construction du groupe national et blanchité dans l'expatriation française à Abu Dhabi." PhD diss., Sciences Po.

Crystal, Jill. 1995. *Oil and Politics in the Gulf: Rulers and Merchants in Kuwait and Qatar*. Cambridge, MA: Cambridge University Press.

Das Gupta, Ashin. 2004. *India and the Indian Ocean World: Trade and Politics*. New Delhi: Oxford University Press.

Davidson, Christopher. 2008. *Dubai: The Vulnerability of Success*. New York: Columbia University Press.

Davis, Mike. 2006. "Fear and Money in Dubai." *New Left Review* 41: 47–68.

Davis, Mike, and Daniel Bertrand Monk. 2007. *Evil Paradises: Dreamworlds of Neoliberalism*. New York: New Press.

De Genova, Nicholas, and Nathalie Peutz. 2010. *The Deportation Regime: Sovereignty, Space, and the Freedom of Movement*. Durham, NC: Duke University Press.

De Regt, Marina. 2010. "Ways to Come, Ways to Leave: Gender, Mobility, and Il/legality among Ethiopian Domestic Workers in Yemen." *Gender & Society* 24 (2): 237–260.

Deeb, Lara, and Mona Harb. 2013. *Leisurely Islam: Negotiating Geography and Morality in Shi'ite South Beirut*. Princeton, NJ: Princeton University Press.

Derderian, Elizabeth. 2019."Displaying Culture: The Politics of Contemporary Art and Liberalism in the UAE." PhD diss., Northwestern University.

DiAngelo, Robin. 2011. "White Fragility." *International Journal of Critical Pedagogy* 3 (3): 54–70.

Diederich, Mathias. 2005. "Indonesians in Saudi Arabia: Religious and Economic Connections." In *Transnational Connections and the Arab Gulf*, edited by Madawi Al Rasheed, 128–146. New York: Routledge.

Doherty, Gareth. 2017. *Paradoxes of Green: Landscapes of a City-State*. Berkeley: University of California Press.

Dresch, Paul. 2000. "Wilderness of Mirrors: Truth and Vulnerability in Middle Eastern Field Work." In *Anthropologists in a Wider World*, edited by Paul Dresch, Wendy James, and David Parkin, 109–128. New York: Berghahn.

Elsheshtawy, Yasser. 2009. *Dubai: Behind an Urban Spectacle*. London: Routledge.

——. 2013. "Resituating the Dubai Spectacle." In *The Superlative City: Dubai and the Urban Condition in the Early Twenty-First Century*, edited by Ahmed Kanna, 104–121. Cambridge, MA: Harvard University Press.

Fabian, Johannes. 1983. *Time and the Other: How Anthropology Makes Its Object*. New York: Columbia University Press.

Farish, Matthew. 2010. *The Contours of America's Cold War*. Minneapolis: University of Minnesota Press.

Fawaz, Mona. 2009. "Neoliberal Urbanity and the Right to the City: A View from Beirut's Periphery." *Development and Change* 40 (5): 827–852.

——. 2014. "The Politics of Property in Planning: Hezbollah's Reconstruction of Haret Hreik (Beirut, Lebanon) as Case Study." *International Journal of Urban and Regional Research* 38 (3): 922–934.

Fechter, Anne-Meike, and Katie Walsh. 2010. "Introduction to Special Issue: Examining 'Expatriate' Continuities: Postcolonial Approaches to Mobile Professionals." *Journal of Ethnic and Migration Studies* 36 (8): 1197–1210.

Federici, Silvia. 2004. *Caliban and the Witch: Women, the Body, and Primitive Accumulation*. Brooklyn, NY: Autonomedia.

——. 2010. *Revolution at Point Zero: Housework, Reproduction, and Feminist Struggle*. Oakland, CA: PM Press.

——. 2019. "On Margaret Benston: The Political Economy of Women's Liberation." *Monthly Review* 71(4): 35–39.

Fennell, Catherine. 2015. *Last Project Standing: Civics and Sympathy in Post-Welfare Chicago*. Minneapolis: University of Minnesota Press.

Ferguson, Roderick A. 2012. *The Reorder of Things: The University and Its Pedagogies of Minority Difference*. Minneapolis: University of Minnesota Press.

Fields, Barbara Jeanne. 1990. "Slavery, Race, and Ideology in the United States of America." *New Left Review* 1 (181): 95–118.

Fields, Karen E., and Barbara J. Fields. 2012. *Racecraft: The Soul of Inequality in American Life*. New York: Verso.

Frankenberg, Ruth. 1993. *White Women, Race Matters: The Social Construction of Whiteness*. Minneapolis: University of Minnesota Press.

Fraser, Nancy. 2014. "Behind Marx's Hidden Abode: For an Expanded Conception of Capitalism." *New Left Review* 86: 55–72.

Fuccaro, Nelida. 2001. "Visions of the City: Urban Studies of the Gulf." *MESA Bulletin* 35: 175–187.

——. 2009. *Histories of City and State in the Persian Gulf: Manama since 1800*. New York: Cambridge University Press.

Gamburd, Michele Ruth. 2000. *The Kitchen Spoon's Handle: Transnationalism and Sri Lanka's Migrant Housemaids*. Ithaca, NY: Cornell University Press.

Gardner, Andrew. 2010. *City of Strangers: Gulf Migration and the Indian Community in Bahrain*. Ithaca, NY: Cornell University Press.

Gregory, Derek. 2004. *The Colonial Present*. Malden MA: Blackwell.

Guha, Ranajit. 1997. *Domination without Hegemony: History and Power in Colonial India*. Cambridge, MA: Harvard University Press.

Günel, Gökçe. 2014. "Ergos: A New Energy Currency." *Anthropological Quarterly* 87 (2): 359–380.

——. 2015. "Electric Potentials: An Interview with Gökçe Günel." Dialogues, *Cultural Anthropology*, November 24, 2015. https://culanth.org/fieldsights/electric-potentials-an-interview-with-g%C3%B6k%C3%A7e-g%C3%BCnel.

——. 2019. *Spaceship in the Desert: Energy, Climate Change, and Urban Design in Abu Dhabi*. Durham, NC: Duke University Press.

Gupta, Akhil, and James Ferguson. 1992. "Beyond 'Culture': Space, Identity, and the Politics of Difference." *Cultural Anthropology* 7 (1): 6–23.

Hammad, Hanan. 2016. *Industrial Sexuality: Gender, Urbanization, and Social Transformation in Egypt*. Austin: University of Texas Press.

Hanieh, Adam. 2011. *Capitalism and Class in the Gulf Arab States*. New York: Palgrave Macmillan.

Hannah, Charity-Anne, Harald Bauder, and John Shields. 2016. "Illegalized Migrant Workers and the Struggle for a Living Wage." *Alternate Routes* 27. http://www.alternateroutes.ca/index.php/ar/article/view/22395.

Haraway, Donna. 1988. "Situated Knowledges: The Science Question in Feminism and the Privilege of Partial Perspective." *Feminist Studies* 14 (3): 575–599.

Harvey, David. 2005. *A Brief History of Neoliberalism*. New York: Oxford University Press.

——. 2008. "The Right to the City." *New Left Review* 53. https://newleftreview.org/II/53/david-harvey-the-right-to-the-city.

——. 2013. *Rebel Cities: From the Right to the City to the Urban Revolution*. New York: Verso.

——. 2014. *Seventeen Contradictions and the End of Capitalism*. New York: Oxford University Press.

Hasso, Frances. 2010. *Consuming Desires: Family Crisis and the State in the Middle East*. Stanford, CA: Stanford University Press.

Ho, Engseng. 2007. *The Graves of Tarim: Genealogy and Mobility across the Indian Ocean.* Berkeley: University of California Press.

Holston, James. 1989. *The Modernist City: An Anthropological Critique of Brasilia.* Chicago: University of Chicago Press.

Hourani, Najib, and Ahmed Kanna. 2014. "Arab Cities in the Neoliberal Moment." *Journal of Urban Affairs* 36 (2): 600–604.

Huber, Matthew T. 2013. *Lifeblood: Oil, Freedom, and the Forces of Capital.* Minneapolis: University of Minnesota Press.

Human Rights Watch. 2006. "Building Towers, Cheating Workers." November 11, 2006. https://www.hrw.org/report/2006/11/11/building-towers-cheating-workers/exploitation-migrant-construction-workers-united.

——. 2014. "United Arab Emirates: Trapped, Exploited, Abused." October 22, 2014. https://www.hrw.org/news/2014/10/22/united-arab-emirates-trapped-exploited-abused.

Ibos, Caroline. 2008. "Les « nounous » africaines et leurs employeurs : Une grammaire du mépris social." *Nouvelles Questions Féministes* 27 (2): 25–38.

Inhorn, Marcia C. 2015. *Cosmopolitan Conceptions: IVF Sojourns in Global Dubai.* Durham, NC: Duke University Press.

Johnson, Mark, and Christoph Wilcke. 2015. "Caged In and Breaking Loose: Intimate Labor, the State, and Migrant Domestic Workers in Saudi Arabia and Other Arab Countries." In *Migrant Encounters: Intimate Labor, the State, and Mobility across Asia*, edited by Sara L. Friedman and Pardis Mahdavi, 135–159. Philadelphia: University of Pennsylvania Press.

Jones, Toby Craig. 2011. *Desert Kingdom: How Oil and Water Forged Modern Saudi Arabia.* Cambridge, MA: Harvard University Press.

Kaminer, Ariel. 2013. "N.Y.U.'s Global Leader Is Tested by Faculty at Home." *New York Times*, May 9, 2013. https://www.nytimes.com/2013/03/10/nyregion/john-sexton-is-tested-by-nyu-faculty.html.

Kanafani, Ghassan. (1962) 1999. *Men in the Sun, and Other Palestinian Stories.* Boulder, CO: Lynne Rienner Publishers.

Kane, Tanya. 2011. "Transplanting Education: A Case Study of the Production of 'American-style' Doctors in a Non-American Setting." *Social Anthropology*, PhD diss., The University of Edinburgh.

Kanna, Ahmed. 2011. *Dubai, the City as Corporation.* Minneapolis: University of Minnesota Press.

——, ed. 2013. *The Superlative City: Dubai and the Urban Condition in the Early XXI Century.* Cambridge, MA: Harvard University Press.

——. 2014. "'A Group of Like-Minded Lads in Heaven': Everydayness and the Production of Dubai Space." *Journal of Urban Affairs* 36: 605–620.

——. 2017. "Gulf Urbanism as a Semantic Field." In *Gateways to the World: Port Cities of the Persian Gulf*, edited by Mehran Kamrava, 79–94. New York: Oxford University Press.

Kelly, Marjorie. 2016. "Richard Serra, Damien Hirst, and Public Art in Qatar." *Public Art Dialogue* 6 (2): 229–240.

Khalaf, Suleyman N. 1992. "Gulf Societies and the Image of Unlimited Good." *Dialectical Anthropology* 17: 53–84.

Khalaf, Suleyman, and Saad Alkobaisi. 1999. "Migrants' Strategies of Coping and Patterns of Accommodation in the Oil-Rich Gulf Societies: Evidence from the UAE." *British Journal of Middle Eastern Studies* 26 (2): 271–298.

Khalifa, Aisha Bikhair. 2006. "African Influence on Culture and Music in Dubai." *International Social Science Journal* 58 (188): 227–235.

Khayyat, Munira, Yasmine Khayyat, and Rola Khayyat. 2018. "Pieces of Us: The Intimate as Imperial Archive." *Journal of Middle East Women's Studies* 14 (3): 268–291.

Knowles, Caroline. 2007. "It's Not What It Was: British Migrants in Postcolonial Hong Kong." *Sociology Working Papers*, 1–25. http://research.gold.ac.uk/8376/.

Koch, Natalie. 2014. "Building Glass Refrigerators in the Desert": Discourses of Urban Sustainability and Nation Building in Qatar." *Urban Geography* 35 (8): 1118–1139.

——. 2015. "Gulf Nationalism and the Geopolitics of Constructing Falconry as a 'Heritage' Sport." *Studies in Ethnicity and Nationalism* 15 (3): 522–539.

——. 2016. "We Entrepreneurial Academics: Creating Spatial Hierarchies and Interpreting Diasporic Academics' Motives to Work in Qatar and the UAE." *Territory, Politics, Governance* 4 (4): 438–452.

——. 2017. "Orientalizing Authoritarianism: Narrating US Exceptionalism in Popular Reactions to the Trump Election and Presidency." *Political Geography*, published online February 28, 2017, https://www.researchgate.net/publication/314286161_Orientalizing_authoritarianism_Narrating_US_exceptionalism_in_popular_reactions_to_the_Trump_election_and_presidency

Koolhaas, Rem. 2006. *The Gulf*. Zürich: Lars Müller.

Kothari, Uma. 2006. "Spatial Practices and Imaginaries: Experience of Colonial Officers and Development Professionals." *Singapore Journal of Tropical Geography* 27 (3): 235–253.

Kracauer, Siegfried. 1995. *The Mass Ornament: Weimar Essays*. Edited and translated by Thomas Y. Levin. Cambridge, MA: Harvard University Press.

Lalami, Feriel. 2008. "L'enjeu du statut des femmes durant la période coloniale en Algérie." *Nouvelles Questions Féministes* 27 (3): 16–27.

Lazzarato, Maurizzio. 2013. *The Making of Indebted Man: An Essay on the Neoliberal Condition*. Translated by Joshua David Jordan. South Pasadena, CA: Semiotext(e).

Le Renard, Amélie. 2011. *Femmes et espaces publics en Arabie Saoudite*. Paris: Dalloz.

——. 2014a. *A Society of Young Women: Opportunities of Place, Power and Reform in Saudi Arabia*. Stanford, CA: Stanford University Press.

——. 2014b. "'On n'est pas formatés comme ça en Occident': Masculinités en compétition, normes de genre et hiérarchies entre nationalités dans une multinationale du Golfe." *Sociétés contemporaines* 94 (2): 41–67.

——. 2016. "'Ici, il y a les Français français et les Français avec origines': Reconfigurations raciales autour d'expériences de Dubaï." *Tracés* 30: 55–78.

——. 2017. "Petits arrangements avec l'égalitarisme: Les Français-e-s de Dubaï et les employées domestiques." *Genèses: Sciences sociales et histoire* 109: 118–138.

——. 2019a. *Le privilège occidental: Travail, intimité et hiérarchies postcoloniales à Dubaï*. Paris: Presses de Sciences Po.

——. 2019b. "Multiple yet Normative: Heterosexual Subjectivities and Western Distinction in Neoliberal Dubai." In *The Everyday Makings of Heteronormativity*, edited by S. Sehlikoglu and F. Kariokis, 121–136. Lanham, MD: Lexington Books.

Lefebvre, Henri. 2003. *The Urban Revolution*. Translated by Robert Bononno. Minneapolis: University of Minnesota Press.

Leonard, Karen. 2003. "South Asian Workers in the Gulf: Jockeying for Places." In *Globalization under Construction*, edited by R. W. Perry and B. Maurer, 129–170. Minneapolis: University of Minnesota Press.

Leonard, Pauline. 2008. "Migrating Identities: Gender, Whiteness, and Britishness in Post-Colonial Hong Kong." *Gender, Place & Culture* 15 (1): 45–60.

———. 2010. *Expatriate Identities in Postcolonial Organizations: Working Whiteness*. Burlington, VT: Routledge.

Lewis, Hannah, Peter Dwyer, Stuart Hodkinson, and Louise Waite. 2015. "Hyperprecarious Lives: Migrants, Work, and Forced Labour in the Global North." *Progress in Human Geography* 39 (5): 580–600.

Lewis, Martin W., and Kären Wigen. 1997. *The Myth of Continents: A Critique of Metageography*. Berkeley: University of California Press.

Lewis, Reina. 1998. *Gendering Orientalism: Race, Femininity and Representation*. New York: Routledge.

———. 2004. *Rethinking Orientalism: Women, Travel, and the Ottoman Harem*. New Brunswick, NJ: Rutgers University Press.

Limbert, Mandana. 2010. *In the Time of Oil: Piety, Memory, and Social Life in an Omani Town*. Palo Alto, CA: Stanford University Press.

———. 2014. "Caste, Ethnicity, and the Politics of Arabness in Southern Arabia." *Comparative Studies of South Asia, Africa and the Middle East* 34 (3): 590–598.

Lindsey, Ursula. 2013. "Qatar Sets Its Own Terms for US Universities." *Chronicle of Higher Education*, November 18, 2013. http://www.chronicle.com/article/Qatar-Welcomes-American/143087.

Lockrem, Jessica, and Adonia Lugo. 2012. "Infrastructure." *Cultural Anthropology* curated collections, November 26, 2012. https://culanth.org/curated_collections/11-infrastructure.

Lombard, Denys, and Jean Aubin, eds. 2000. *Asian Merchants and Businessmen in the Indian Ocean and the China Sea*. New Delhi: Oxford University Press.

Longva, Ahn Nga. 1997. *Walls Built on Sand: Migration, Exclusion, and Society in Kuwait*. Boulder, CO: Westview Press.

———. 2005. "Neither Autocracy nor Democracy but Ethnocracy: Citizens, Expatriates and the Sociopolitical System in Kuwait." In *Monarchies and Nations*, edited by P. Dresch and J. Piscatori, 114–135. London: I. B. Tauris.

Lori, Noora. 2011. "National Security and the Management of Migrant Labor: A Case Study of the United Arab Emirates." *Asian and Pacific Migration Journal* 20 (3–4): 315–337.

———. 2012. *Temporary Workers or Permanent Migrants? The Kafala System and Contestations over Residency in the Arab Gulf States*. Paris: Ifri, Center for Migrations and Citizenship.

Low, Setha M. 2000. *On the Plaza: The Politics of Public Space and Culture*. Austin: University of Texas Press.

Lowe, Lisa. 2015. *The Intimacies of Four Continents*. Durham, NC: Duke University Press.

Lundström, Catrin. 2014. *White Migrations: Gender, Whiteness and Privilege in Transnational Migration*. Basingstoke: Palgrave Macmillan.

Lutz, Catherine, ed. 2009. *The Bases of Empire: The Global Struggle against U.S. Military Posts*. New York: NYU Press.

MacLean, Nancy. 2017. *Democracy in Chains: The Deep History of the Radical Right's Stealth Plan for America*. New York: Penguin.

MacNeill, Donald. 2009. *The Global Architect: Firms, Fame, and Urban Form*. New York: Routledge.

Mahdavi, Pardis. 2011. *Gridlock: Labor, Migration, and Human Trafficking in Dubai*. Stanford, CA: Stanford University Press.

——. 2013. "Gender, Labor and the Law: The Nexus of Domestic Work, Human Trafficking, and the Informal Economy in the United Arab Emirates." *Global Networks* 13 (4): 425–440.

——. 2016. *Crossing the Gulf: Love and Family in Migrant Lives*. Stanford, CA: Stanford University Press.

Mahmud, Lilith. 2016. "We Have Never Been Liberal: Occidentalist Myths and the Impending Fascist Apocalypse." *Hot Spots, Cultural Anthropology*, October 27, 2016. https://culanth.org/fieldsights/we-have-never-been-liberal-occidentalist-myths-and-the-impending-fascist-apocalypse.

Mains, Daniel. 2012. "Blackouts and Progress: Privatization, Infrastructure, and a Developmentalist State in Jimma, Ethiopia." *Cultural Anthropology* 27 (1): 3–27.

Maira, Sunaina Marr. 2009. *Missing: Youth, Citizenship, and Empire after 9/11*. Durham, NC: Duke University Press.

Malecki, Edward J., and Michael C. Ewers. 2007. "Labor Migration to World Cities: With a Research Agenda for the Arab Gulf." *Progress in Human Geography* 31 (4): 467–484.

Malik, Nesrine. 2009. "The 'Virtual Slaves' of the Gulf States." *Guardian*, November 16, 2009. https://www.theguardian.com/commentisfree/2009/nov/16/gulf-states-asian-workers-rights.

Mamdani, Mahmood. 2004. *Good Muslim, Bad Muslim: America, the Cold War, and the Roots of Terror*. New York: Three Leaves Press.

Mankekar, Purnima. 1999. "Brides Who Travel: Gender, Transnationalism, and Nationalism in Hindi Film." *Positions* 7 (3): 731–761.

Marchal, Roland. 2005. "Dubai: Global City and Transnational Hub." In *Transnational Connections and the Arab Gulf*, edited by Madawi Al Rasheed, 93–110. New York: Routledge.

Marx, Karl. 1976. *Capital: Volume 1*. Translated by Ben Fowkes. New York: Penguin.

Mathew, Johan. 2016. *Margins of the Market: Trafficking and Capitalism across the Arabian Sea*. Oakland: University of California Press.

Matthiesen, Toby. 2013. *Sectarian Gulf: Bahrain, Saudi Arabia, and the Arab Spring That Wasn't*. Stanford, CA: Stanford University Press.

——. 2014. *The Other Saudis: Shiism, Dissent and Sectarianism*. New York: Cambridge University Press.

Melman, Billie. 1992. *Women's Orients: English Women and the Middle East, 1718–1918: Sexuality, Religion and Work*. London: Palgrave Macmillan.

Menoret, Pascal. 2005. *The Saudi Enigma: A History*. Translated by Patrick Camiller. New York: Zed Books.

———. 2011. "Leaving Islamic Activism Behind: Ambiguous Disengagement in Saudi Arabia." In *Social Movements, Mobilization and Contestation in the Middle East and North Africa*, edited by Joel Beinin and Frédéric Vairel, 43–60. Palo Alto, CA: Stanford University Press.

———. 2014. *Joyriding in Riyadh: Oil, Urbanism, and Road Revolt.* New York: Cambridge University Press.

Mignolo, Walter. 2002. "The Geopolitics of Knowledge and Colonial Difference." *South Atlantic Quarterly* 101 (1): 57–96.

Mitchell, Kevin. 2015. "Design for the Future: Educational Institutions in the Gulf" *Architectural Design: Special Issue: UAE and The Gulf: Architecture and Urbanism* 85(1): 38–45.

Mitchell, Timothy. 1991. *Colonising Egypt.* Berkeley: University of California Press.

———. 2011. *Carbon Democracy: Political Power in the Age of Oil.* New York: Verso Books.

Moghadam, Amin. 2013. "De l'Iran imaginé aux nouveaux foyers de l'Iran: Pratiques et espaces transnationaux des Iraniens à Dubaï." *Arabian Humanities* 2. http://cy.revues.org/2556.

Mohanty, Chandra Talpade. 1984. "Under Western Eyes: Feminist Scholarship and Colonial Discourses." *Boundary* 2: 333–358.

Munif, Abdul Rahman. 1987. *Cities of Salt.* New York: Vintage Books.

———. 1991. *The Trench.* New York: Vintage Books.

———. 1993. *Variations on Night and Day.* New York: Vintage Books.

Nagy, Sharon. 2008. "The Search for Miss Philippines Bahrain—Possibilities for Representation in Expatriate Communities." *City & Society* 20 (1): 79–104.

Najmabadi, Afsaneh. 2005. *Women without Mustaches and Men without Beards, Gender and Sexual Anxiety of Iranian Modernity.* Berkeley: University of California Press.

Narayan, Kirin. 1993. "How Native Is a 'Native' Anthropologist?" *American Anthropologist* 95 (3): 671–686.

Navarro, Tami, Bianca Williams, and Attiya Ahmad. 2013. "Sitting at the Kitchen Table: Fieldnotes from Women of Color in Anthropology." *Cultural Anthropology* 28 (3): 443–463.

Newman, Andrew. 2015. *Landscape of Discontent: Urban Sustainability in Immigrant Paris.* Minneapolis: University of Minnesota Press.

Ollus, Natalia. 2016. "Forced Flexibility and Exploitation: Experiences of Migrant Workers in the Cleaning Industry." *Nordic Journal of Working Life Studies* 6 (1): 25–45.

Ong, Aihwa. 1999. *Flexible Citizenship: The Cultural Logics of Transnationality.* Durham, NC: Duke University Press.

Onley, James. 2007. *The Arabian Frontier of the British Raj: Merchants, Rulers, and the British in the Nineteenth-Century Gulf.* New York: Oxford University Press.

Osella, Caroline, and Filippo Osella. 2006. "Once Upon a Time in the West: Stories of Migration and Modernity from Kerala, South India." *Journal of the Royal Anthropological Institute* 12 (3): 569–588.

Parreñas, Rhacel Salazar. 2000. "Migrant Filipina Domestic Workers and the International Division of Reproductive Labor." *Gender and Society* 14 (4): 560–580.

Peterson, Marina, and Gary McDonogh. 2012. *Global Downtowns*. Philadelphia: University of Pennsylvania Press.

Peutz, Nathalie. 2011. "Bedouin 'Abjection': World Heritage, Worldliness, and Worthiness at the Margins of Arabia." *American Ethnologist* 38 (2): 338–360.

Puar, Jasbir. 2007. *Terrorist Assemblages: Homonationalism in Queer Times*. Durham, NC: Duke University Press.

Quijano, Anibal. 2000. "Coloniality of Power, Eurocentrism, and Latin America." *Nepentla: Views from the South* 1 (3): 533–580.

Rahman, Anisur. 2001. *Indian Labour Migration to the Gulf: A Socio-Economic Analysis*. New Delhi: Rajat Publications.

Ramesh, Randeep. 2017. "The Long-Running Family Rivalries behind the Qatar Crisis." *Guardian*, July 21, 2017. https://www.theguardian.com/world/2017/jul/21/qatar-crisis -may-be-rooted-in-old-family-rivalries.

Ramos, Stephen J. 2010. *Dubai Amplified: The Engineering of a Port Geography*. Surrey, UK: Ashgate.

Ramos, Stephen, and Peter G. Rowe. 2013. "Planning, Prototyping, and Replication in Dubai." In *The Superlative City: Dubai and the Urban Condition in the Early Twenty-First Century*, edited by Ahmed Kanna, 18–33. Cambridge, MA: Harvard University Press.

Readings, Bill. 1996. *The University in Ruins*. Cambridge, MA: Harvard University Press.

Ridge, Natasha. 2014. *Education and the Reverse Gender Divide in the Gulf States*. New York: Teachers College Press.

Ross, Andrew. 2011. "Human Rights, Academic Freedom, and Offshore Academics." American Association of University Professors. January–February 2011. https://www .aaup.org/article/human-rights-academic-freedom-and-offshore-academics# .WZ8pplKZNao.

Rotenberg, Robert. 1995. *Landscape and Power in Vienna*. Baltimore: Johns Hopkins University Press.

Said, Edward. 1978. *Orientalism*. New York: Pantheon Books.

Samiei, Mohammad. 2010. "Neo-Orientalism? The Relationship between the West and Islam in Our Globalised World." *Third World Quarterly* 31 (7): 1145–1160.

Samin, Nadav. 2015. *Of Sand or Soil: Genealogy and Tribal Belonging in Saudi Arabia*. Princeton, NJ: Princeton University Press.

Sekher, T. V. 1997. *Migration and Social Change*. Jaipur: Rawat Publications.

Shehabi, Ala'a, and Marc Owen Jones. 2015. *Bahrain's Uprising*. London: Zed Books.

Thiollet, Hélène. 2010. "Nationalisme d'État et nationalisme ordinaire en Arabie Saoudite: La nation saoudienne et ses immigrés." *Raisons politiques* 37: 89–101.

Thiollet, Hélène, and Leïla Vignal. 2016. "Transnationalising the Arabian Peninsula: Local, Regional and Global Dynamics." *Arabian Humanities* 7. http://journals .openedition.org/cy/3145.

Trawrî, Mahmûd. 2007. *Maymûna*. Damascus: Al-Mada.

Ulrichsen, Kristian Coates. 2014. *Qatar and the Arab Spring*. New York: Oxford University Press.

Vitalis, Robert. 2007. *America's Kingdom: Mythmaking on the Saudi Oil Frontier*. Palo Alto, CA: Stanford University Press.

Vogel, Carol. 2013. "Art, from Conception to Birth in Qatar." *New York Times*, October 7, 2013. http://www.nytimes.com/2013/10/08/arts/design/damien-hirsts-anatomical -sculptures-have-their-debut.html?mcubz=3&mtrref=www.google.com&gwh=0A74 2C461173E59871FA447EE7AEE574&gwt=pay.

Vogel, Lise. 2013. *Marxism and the Oppression of Women: Toward a Unitary Theory*. Chicago: Haymarket Books.

——. 2019. "She Was My Kind of Scientist: Margaret Benston and the Political Economy of Women's Liberation." *Monthly Review* 71(4): 12–22.

Vogel, Richard D. 2006. "Harder Times: Undocumented Workers and the U.S. Informal Economy." *Monthly Review* 58 (3). https://monthlyreview.org/2006/07/01/harder -times-undocumented-workers-and-the-u-s-informal-economy/.

——. 2007. "Transient Servitude: The U.S. Guest Worker Program for Exploiting Mexican and Central American Workers." *Monthly Review* 58 (8). https://monthlyreview.org /2007/01/01/transient-servitude-the-u-s-guest-worker-program-for-exploiting-mexican -and-central-american-workers/.

Vora, Neha. 2012. "Free Speech and Civil Discourse: Producing Expats, Locals, and Migrants in the UAE English-Language Blogosphere." *Journal of the Royal Anthropological Institute* 18 (4): 787–807.

——. 2013a. *Impossible Citizens: Dubai's Indian Diaspora*. Durham, NC: Duke University Press.

——. 2013b. "Theorizing the Arabian Peninsula Roundtable: Unpacking Knowledge Production and Consumption." Jadaliyya. April 22, 2013. http://www.jadaliyya.com /pages/index/11296/theorizing-the-arabian-peninsula-roundtable_unpack.

——. 2014a. "Between Global Citizenship and Qatarization: Negotiating Qatar's New Knowledge Economy within American Branch Campuses." *Ethnic & Racial Studies* 37 (12): 2243–2260.

——. 2014b. "Expat/Expert Camps: Redefining Labor within Gulf Migration." In *Transit States: Labour, Migration & Citizenship in the Gulf*, edited by Omar l-Shehabi, Adam Hanieh, and Abdulhadi Khalaf, 170–197. New York: Pluto Press.

——. 2015. "Is the University Universal? Mobile (Re)Constitutions of American Academia in the Gulf Arab States." *Anthropology & Education Quarterly* 46 (1): 19–36.

——. 2018. *Teach for Arabia: American Universities, Liberalism, and Transnational Qatar*. Stanford, CA: Stanford University Press.

Vora, Neha, and Ahmed Kanna. 2018. "De-exceptionalizing the Field: Anthropological Reflections on Migration, Labor, and Identity in Dubai." *Arab Studies Journal* 26 (2): 74–100.

Vora, Neha, and Natalie Koch. 2015. "Everyday Inclusions: Rethinking Ethnocracy, *Kafala*, and Belonging in the GCC." *Studies in Ethnicity and Nationalism* 15 (3): 540–552.

Walsh, Katie. 2006. "'Dad Says I'm Tied to a Shooting Star!' Grounding (Research on) British Expatriate Belonging." *Area* (38): 268–278.

——. 2007. "It Got Very Debauched, Very Dubai!" Heterosexual Intimacy amongst Single British Expatriates." *Social & Cultural Geography* 8 (4): 507–533.

——. 2010. "Negotiating Migrant Status in the Emerging Global City: Britons in Dubai." *Encounters*: 235–255.

———. 2012. "Travelling Together? Work, Intimacy, and Home amongst British Expatriate Couples in Dubai." In *Gender and Family among Transnational Professionals*, edited by Ann Coles and Anne-Meike Fechter, 63–84. New York: Routledge.

Weber, Charlotte. 2001. "Unveiling Scheherazade: Feminist Orientalism in the International Alliance of Women, 1911–1950." *Feminist Studies* 27 (1): 125–157.

Wilhelm, Ian. 2011. "Duke Faculty Question the University's Global Ambitions." *Chronicle of Higher Education* 58 (11). http://www.chronicle.com/article/Duke-Faculty -Question-the/129536.

Willis, John M. 2013. *Unmaking North and South: Cartographies of the Yemeni Past.* New York: Columbia/Hurst.

Wise, Raul Delgado. 2013. "The Migration and Labor Question Today: Imperialism, Unequal Development, and Forced Migration." *Monthly Review* 64 (9). https:// monthlyreview.org/2013/02/01/the-migration-and-labor-question-today-imperialism -unequal-development-and-forced-migration/.

Wright, Andrea. 2015. "Migratory Pipelines: Labor and Oil in the Arabian Sea." PhD diss., University of Michigan.

Yegenoglu, Meyda. 1998. *Colonial Fantasies: Towards a Feminist Reading of Orientalism.* Cambridge: Cambridge University Press.

Zhang, Li. 2001. *Strangers in the City: Reconfigurations of Space, Power, and Social Networks within China's Floating Population.* Stanford, CA: Stanford University Press.

Index